COOKING

for

College Students

A Beginner's Guide

Cooking for College Students
A Beginner's Guide

PATRICK C. ARENSON

NewtonLocke.com

The Internet's Premiere Site for Undiscovered Talent
Everywhere, USA

www.thestinc.com

For information about special discounts for schools, ordering, or cooking classes,
please write to patrickarenson@bellsouth.net

Published by NewtonLocke.com,
The Internet's Premiere Site for Undiscovered Talent

Arenson, Patrick C.
The College Cookbook: A Beginner's Guide/ by Patrick C. Arenson

Third American Edition, September 2011

For everyone who has ever given me food. I wrote this book for my friends to help you guys learn how to cook, so I expect each and every one of you to reciprocate the effort by being on street corners with fluorescent vests and flyers, hustling this book to strangers as if your lives depended on it. I'm talking about 16 hours a day, weekends, holidays, bar mitzvahs and baby showers. If not, you can forget about those outrageously expensive shoes with the red bottom, that beach house in Sausalito, dinner at El Bulli and the French Laundry, the trip to Amsterdam...Just kidding. You guys are awesome and I wouldn't have been able to do this without you. (PS I have eyes everywhere).

BTW:

I decided to print this book in black and white so it could be affordable for everyone. I hope to have full color editions soon. Please visit www.thestinc.com for the latest information.

TABLE OF CONTENTS

INTRODUCTION

The idea behind this book came to me one afternoon during summer vacation, a couple days after my sister had returned home from college.

"I think you should write me a cookbook," she told me suddenly.

"What?!"

I wanted to laugh because my sister was perhaps the last person I would ever imagine toiling over a hot stove. She hated doing dishes, let alone cooking, and so I had to wonder whether or not she was still recovering from her organic-chemistry filled spring semester, and if this was just a cry for help.

But she was serious, and as someone who would find a challenge of this magnitude appealing, I took her seriously. *Stupid, stupid!*

"I want you to teach me how to cook," she continued, "and then *we* can write it down so I can make it when I go back to school." She genuinely looked like she was expecting something hardbound and gift wrapped for her at the end of the summer. *Mom*, I thought to myself, *Ashley needs to be examined. Now!*

But I couldn't resist the idea, and my curiosity was overwhelming.

"Why?"

Shut up, Patrick! You're digging your own grave!

"Because I'm tired of eating the same things over and over again and I can't go out every night. I need you to teach me how to cook."

Speechlessness is a curious thing for someone like me, but in that instant, the heavens opened and God threw down a frying pan that hit me square across the face.

I wrote Cooking for College Students to teach people how to cook delicious and simple food. But I was a college student myself and I had heard of cooking horror stories and even seen firsthand what a dorm room looked like after making a simple snack. So if I was going to change every how college students ate, I had my work cut out for me.

Before I even began writing, I had already thought of the book I wanted to write. I wanted something that could be useful to everyone who picked it up, something that could help college students save money on takeout and fast food, something that might even replace the dining hall (at least a couple times a week). So I asked my friends what kind of food they liked, and from that, I created recipes that could be made with just a handful of budget friendly ingredients, recipes that would need as little input as possible and best of all, recipes that would require very little clean up afterwards. I wanted all the dishes to be able to feed a crowd as easily as two people and because I hate leftovers, I wanted to turn old dishes into exciting new ones.

Most importantly, I knew the food had to be great! Many of these recipes are reinvented, simplified versions of my favorite dishes from restaurants, tricks that I had developed into saving money when I wanted to go out. You don't have to eat out every day to have a great meal, and you don't have to spend a fortune for great food either.

Cooking for College Students: A Beginner's Guide is a collection of some of my favorite recipes all catered to the college lifestyle. With weekly menus and shopping lists to get you through the week, and instructions on everything from basic preparations to knife skills to buying the best ingredients and using up leftovers, I hope this book is as much of a manual and instruction guide as it is a vehicle to encourage people to get more interested in cooking.

College is all about new experiences and food is one of the best ways to trigger memories so I hope you think of this book ten years down the line, as you're making the 3 minute hot chocolate cake or the Asian pizza, and it takes you back to some of the best days of your life.

Dear Students,

Please fill out the following form.

I _____ (owner of the book) do hereby solemnly swear that I will learn how to cook, upon severe pain of hunger (death). I will NOT continue to buy bad, overpriced food at _____ (restaurant), _____ (restaurant) or _____ (restaurant) and I will not spend $_____ (number) a week on things that I can make at home.

I will try to make healthy food choices and buy fresh, seasonal ingredients. I will not cook every day, but I will try and cook at least _____ (number) times a week.

Last year, I spent about $_____ (number) on food, and at the end of the year, my goal is to save $_____ (number) on my food budget and impress _____ (person) with my amazing cooking skills. I want to become a great chef like _____ (write Patrick Arenson, just kidding).

I will also tell _____ (friend), _____ (friend) and _____ (friend) about this book, because they desperately need to learn how to cook. And with the money I will be saving, I will use it to _____ (your dream).

Signature: _____   Date: _____

Thanks,

Patrick C. Arenson

SHOPPING LIST

- LARGE OVEN SAFE PAN, NON STICK PREFERABLE

  Purchase one that has high sides and a lid so that it can be used to braise and stew ingredients, even if it is never used to do so- the high sides will help reduce the mess. The one I own is about 14 inches in diameter that I bought on sale for $15 dollars. The best ones are made of stainless steel or enameled. Before you purchase one, lay it on the ground to make sure it lies completely flat because sometimes you'll find cheaper ones that aren't worth their trouble. And remember, the heavier the pan, the better it is.

- LARGE STOCK POT

  Purchase a pot made from stainless steel that is larger than 3 quarts but smaller than 6 quarts. Make sure there is a lid included.

- STRAINER

  Any large strainer will do and some come included with the stock pot. If you can get a deal, do it.

- BAKING SHEET

  Buy a nonstick one if possible.

- CHEF'S KNIFE

  Purchasing a chef's knife is more about comfort than anything. My recommendation is to purchase a 6 or 7 inch chef's knife. If you are less experienced, I would highly recommend the smaller of the two. It will be the only knife you will ever need, so pick something comfortable, durable and reputable (but not necessarily expensive).

- CUTTING BOARD

  If possible, get one with small grooves on the side, which will catch the juice from the meat as it is being sliced. I prefer wooden cutting boards over plastic cutting boards because plastic cutting boards tend to stain. Some people also don't think it's hygienic to prepare raw chicken on the wooden board, but its fine: just clean it after each use.

- A SET OF MEASURING CUPS

  Buy an inexpensive dry measuring cup set, and if necessary, it can be used for liquids as well. If you can find a metal set, you can also use it directly on the stove to cook eggs.

- WOODEN SPOON

  Invented by the cavemen, there still is no better stirring object in the world, except for your hands; but if we're talking about stirring something in a pan, maybe we'll stick to the spoon and get a rain check on the first degree burns.

- KITCHEN TONGS

  Although this item may seem unnecessary, it will be very useful for picking up meat and pulling out hot items from the oven.

- METAL SPATULA

- A CAFETERA

  Also known as a Cuban coffee maker, it's about six dollars for a 3 cup coffee maker, and it will save you about $2 a day, every day for 4 years.

- OVEN MITS AND KITCHEN TOWELS

  Buy a lot of cheap kitchen towels; they are essential because there will probably be a messy counter afterwards and the towels can serve many purposes. They're better than having to use your dirty shirt, especially if the ketchup stain doesn't come out in the wash. If the kitchen towels are thick enough, they can also double as oven mits.

- TWO LARGE MIXING BOWLS, ONE THAT IS MICROWAVABLE

  Buy one that can fit in the other. Chances are only one will be used for the recipe, but in the event that both are needed, it's good to have an option. The microwavable one can be used to make rice and when you're done, you can stack them and store them together.

- WATER FILTER

  Buy a water filter system (like Brita) that you simply fill up with tap water and put into the refrigerator. Many campuses don't have fresh water and it will save you a lot of aggravation when you don't have to buy water bottles from the store every week.

- REUSABLE WATER BOTTLE

  They are more cost efficient than regular water bottles and they are better for the environment. Check the manufacturing labels because some companies use questionable materials in their production.

- PLATES, UTENSILS (make sure to get tablespoons and teaspoons), BOWLS AND MUGS. If you're Asian, get chopsticks and you've just saved yourself a hell of a lot of dishes.

- LARGE RECLOSABLE CONTAINERS for cereal, sugar, coffee, flour etc.

- TUPPERWARE

  Your parents' tupperware will probably end up in your kitchen with all the food they'll send from home, so this isn't a priority.

- VEGETABLE PEELER

  Any regular vegetable peeler can also double as a cheese grater.

SPLURGE

If your parents are feeling generous (and at this point they might as well should be because they are already spending a lot of money sending you to school), purchase these in addition to what is already listed.

- ENAMELED CAST IRON SKILLET (This is an upgrade on the nonstick)

  Enameled cast iron skillets are superior to our other nonstick pans because they retain heat very well and last forever. The most sought after (and expensive) ones are by Le Creuset, but Cuisinart and other companies make excellent ones as well. *This will replace the regular non stick pan* and will probably last long enough to give it to your child in twenty years (along with a copy of this book, cough, cough!)

- BLENDER

  A blender can be used for a lot of different things from pureeing vegetables to making smoothies. Most probably, it will be used for making frozen drinks, but it can also make vinaigrettes and really quick soups. My friend owns a Magic Bullet that is really great for making drinks… I mean pureed vegetable soups and smoothies.

- SERVING PLATTER

  Only one is necessary. Buy a large white one that can be used for a lot of people, especially during game nights.

- CUPCAKE PANS

  For birthdays- I know a lot of my friends (all of them girls) who give each other cup cakes and brownies for birthdays. But I'm not a baker, so I usually end up at the grocery store.

- CHEESE GRATER

  Although you can certainly buy already grated cheese in the store, this is better.

WHERE TO SHOP?

Shopping for good cooking supplies can be very difficult because some items are so specific that there really is no incentive to put them on sale. For the best cooking supplies, shop at **William-Sonoma**, which can satisfy almost all of your cooking related needs. Unfortunately, some items can be very expensive, so I almost always take a very doting family member when I visit.

Whenever I shop for cooking supplies, I always go to stores like **Marshall's** and **TJ Maxx**. My favorite store is Marshall's: They have everything you need (all excellent quality) at prices that will beat out every single competitor. I also advise that you look in the clearance section and poke around. *Many stores will reduce prices even more if you find even slightly damaged items, so ask for a discount.* Marshall's also has white truffle oil. If you see it, buy it to drizzle on pasta, bread or some sides. If you don't know what to do with it, send it to me.

For items you can't find at Marshalls, go to **Macys** or **Sears**.

When you're grocery shopping for meat, try to buy in bulk. You can't get any better quality than **Costco** or **BJ's**. Simply separate everything into storage bags when you get home from the grocery store and place them in the freezer. Then all you need it to defrost the meat when you are ready to cook.

For grocery stores, **Trader Joes** optimizes amazing quality and price. We just don't have them in Miami. For organic, **Whole Foods** and **Fresh Market** seem to be the leading contenders but they are also the most expensive.

PANTRY MUST-HAVES

- Garlic
- Onions
- Nuts (cashews, walnuts, pecans, peanuts)
- Peanut Butter
- Cooking Spray
- Vegetable oil
- Olive oil
- Balsamic Vinegar
- Chicken/beef stock or bouillon cubes
- Ketchup
- Mustard
- Salsa
- Tabasco Sauce
- Honey Barbeque Sauce
- Rice
- Black Beans
- Chickpeas or Garbanzo Beans
- Salad wraps
- Pita bread
- Pasta
- All purpose flour
- Panko bread crumbs
- Sugar
- Soy sauce
- Crushed tomatoes
- Tomato Paste
- Oat meal

GREAT ADDITIONS

- Toasted Sesame oil
- *White truffle oil
- White beans
- Thai sweet chili sauce/sweet and sour sauce
- Fresh basil and rosemary

FRIDGE OR FREEZER

- Butter
- Milk
- Pizza dough
- Fresh fruit and vegetables (see pg.49)
- Frozen corn, peas, spinach, carrots
- Yogurt
- Soda/Juice
- Eggs
- Bread
- Parmesan cheese
- Bacon
- Defrosted Chicken breasts
- Ground coffee

BUY ON SALE AND STORE

- Ground Beef
- Steaks
- Deli meats like ham and cheese

SNACKS

- Cereal
- Granola bars/cereal bar
- Something frozen like ice cream or fruit bars
- A small bag of cookies
- Hot dogs
- Pretzels
- Cheese
- Wheat Thins
- Chocolate chips
- Craisins

SPICE RACK

- Salt
- Pepper
- Rosemary
- Thyme
- Basil

Secondary Spices

- Paprika
- Garlic Powder
- Sage
- Curry Powder

OVER 21

- Red wine
- Beer
- Vodka

THINGS YOU SHOULD ALWAYS BUY AND NEVER MAKE

When I began planning recipes for this book, I was extremely conscious about prices and the number of ingredients per recipe. As I progressed, I noticed that some things were better to buy than make, and others should never be bought at all. This list will save you a lot of time and money at the grocery story.

- Hummus (they have good sundried tomato varieties that are cheaper than if you were to buy the sundried tomatoes by themselves)
- French Fries (buy them in the frozen food aisle and save yourself a lot of work)
- Potato chips
- Salsa
- Granola
- Gnocchi
- Cakes, Pies, Cheesecakes, etc. (grocery stores have a great selection, and if you were to buy all the components to make a chocolate cake, you would spend over $15 when you can buy a professionally made one for about $10)
- Cookies (if you didn't have any of the ingredients beforehand)
- Jarred tomato sauce (you don't always have to make your own)
- Pizza dough and any type of bread (I don't think anyone's going to try to make pizza dough, but trust me, it's a pain)

THINGS YOU SHOULD NEVER BUY FROM THE STORE

- Premade or frozen burgers (they are disgusting and expensive)
- Pre-seasoned meat of any kind (either make it at home, or get take out)
- Premade Alfredo sauce
- Precooked bacon (how lazy can you get)
- Fresh pasta (it's overpriced and is really bad quality)
- Bottled Water (buy a water bottle and a filter)
- Brick chocolate (it is an extremely expensive version of chocolate chips)
- Pre sliced fruits or vegetables (unless it's a watermelon, do it yourself)
- Boxed macaroni and cheese (the version in this book is actually cheaper, tastier and serves 6-8 people)

OVERPRICED THINGS YOU CAN MAKE AT HOME INSTEAD OF BUYING

- Parfaits (its yogurt and granola)
- Coffee (in any of its forms)
- Milkshakes
- Smoothies (use yogurt or frozen fruit)
- Sandwiches (You can make a sandwich that's twice as good as the ones they have at subway, with better ingredients and at half the price)
- Pasta
- Salads

MISTAKES TO LEARN FROM

- TASTE AND SEASON AS YOU GO.

This is singlehandedly the biggest problem that beginning chefs have. Whenever you are making a recipe, taste it every step of the way and adjust the seasoning as necessary. And remember, if you are reducing something, don't add too much salt because it will intensify later.

- DON'T TRY TO TAKE ADDITIONAL SHORTCUTS!

This is not the book where you want to omit ingredients or take shortcuts because I've already done that for you! If you do, you won't end up with the same product. Also, don't rush through a recipe because you leave yourself more open to mistakes.

- RESTRAIN YOURSELF

I know there is a temptation to want to press down on burgers, to constantly flip chicken or open up the oven. The truth is, you don't want to handle your food too much because it ends up slowing you down in the long run.

- AND FINALLY, CLEAN AS YOU GO!

APPROACHING THE WEEK

Cooking at home is truly a great way to make college life better, and it makes it a lot cheaper too. I wanted to include some weekly menus, all based on recipes found in this book, to help simplify your life and eliminate the mystery about what's for dinner. In addition, here are some tricks to making your life easier and your food better.

- MARINATE OR BRINE

Marinating and brining are techniques that use seasoning to heighten the flavor over time. As soon as you get home from the grocery story, separate your meat into single portion plastic freezer bags and season them before you put them into the fridge or freezer. Then all you have to remember is to take the food out of the freezer the night before, and the next day, it's already defrosted and ready to cook. IT WILL TASTE SO MUCH BETTER THIS WAY!

- USE YOUR LEFTOVERS

These recipes were written to make great use of the leftovers. If you use things like side dishes from the night before, all you have to do is make the main course and you'll have a complete meal in half the time.

- ANTICIPATE THE HEATING-UP TIME

Preheat the oven and boil the water as soon as you step through the door, because they take about 10 minutes to get up to the right temperature.

- MEALS ARE PROTEIN, SIDES AND VEGETABLE

Depending on what is on sale at the store, buy two or three different proteins every week, separate them into individual plastic bags when you get home and then you'll have at least one type of meat ready to be cooked at a moment's notice. Side dishes like rice, pasta and couscous are great to buy in bulk and store because they don't require refrigeration.

- MOST OF ALL, DON'T COOK EVERY DAY

Even I don't cook everyday- sometimes you don't have time, or just don't want to, so every once in a while, go out or order a pizza, and when the time comes that you have to cook, it doesn't feel like a chore.

WEEKLY MENU 1

	Breakfast	Lunch	Dinner
Monday	One Eyed Sandwich	Tacos	9 Spice Chicken
Tuesday	Oatmeal	Mexican Pasta (leftover taco meat)	Pineapple Express Fried Rice (leftover white rice)
Wednesday	Cereal	Skirt Steak With Sautéed Broccoli	Chicken Quesadilla (leftover chicken)
Thursday	Fried Egg	Salad with honey balsamic dressing	Steak sandwich (leftover steak) with summer corn salad
Friday	Smoothie	Go Out	Marinated Pork Loin with Wasabi mashed potatoes
Saturday	Omelet with bruschetta and cheese	Pan con Lechon (leftover pork)	Roasted Tomato Soup with Grilled Cheese
Sunday	Go Out		Sweet and Sour Chicken

Base Protein: Ground beef, pork, skirt steak and boneless skinless chicken breast, eggs

WEEKLY MENU 2

	Breakfast	Lunch	Dinner
Monday	Pancakes	Chicken Milanese	Spaghetti and Meatballs
Tuesday	Cereal	Sandwich	Mini burgers with twice baked potatoes
Wednesday	George Foreman French Toast (leftover bread)	Meatball sub (leftover meatballs)	Crispy Chicken Salad (leftover chicken Milanese)
Thursday	Oatmeal	9 Spice Chicken	Steak au poivre (with creamed spinach)
Friday	Eggs and Bacon	Go out.	Cuban Pitza
Saturday	Smoothie	Mongolian beef (leftover steak)	Go out.
Sunday		Brunch- Breakfast Carbonara	Leftovers

Proteins: Ground beef, boneless skinless chicken breast, skirt steak or New York Strip steak, eggs.

WEEKLY MENU 3

	Breakfast	Lunch	Dinner
Monday	Bagels	Sausage with Pepper and Onions	Pollo a la Plancha with white rice
Tuesday	George Foreman French Toast	Shrimp with Garlic oil	20 Minute Pasta
Wednesday	Pan tostada	Pineapple express fried rice (leftover rice)	Nachos (leftover chicken and shrimp)
Thursday	Oatmeal and café con leche	Shrimp Scampi	Go Out
Friday	Cereal	Go Out	Asian Pizza (leftover sweet and sour chicken) 3 minute chocolate cake
Saturday	Smoothie	Salad with crispy chicken	Shrimp Quesadilla
Sunday	Go Out	Sausage and Beer hoagies	Pitza

Base Proteins: shrimp, boneless skinless chicken breast and sausage.

Breakfast

Pancakes

MATERIALS
A non stick pan
2 bowls
Spatula
A fork
Measuring cup

INGREDIENTS
1 cup of flour
2 eggs
Pinch salt
One 6 oz container of Fruit on the Bottom yogurt or 2/3 cup sour cream

4 tablespoons sugar or sugar substitute
1 tablespoon butter
2/3 cup milk
1 teaspoon baking powder
Cooking spray
1 teaspoon vanilla (optional)

"Wait! What is that? No! Stop! What are you doing!"

The first time my friends saw me make pancakes, they quickly became squeamish like little rats, especially when I pulled the sour cream out of the fridge. They couldn't understand that the sour cream was responsible for making the pancakes ultra light and soft. Even now, they're still confused.

In case you don't have sour cream, use fruit on the bottom yogurt (it's made by Dannon).

20 minutes

BATTER: In one bowl, combine the flour, salt, sugar and baking powder. In another, combine the eggs, yogurt and milk. Mix together until you are left with a smooth batter.

COOK: Heat up the nonstick pan to medium high. Add ½ a tablespoon of butter with a quick spray of cooking spray. Add a quarter of the batter to the pan and cook for 2 to 3 minutes. The pancakes should have bubbles around the entire edge and the underside should be stiff when you try to lift it. Then it is ready to flip.

Flip the pancake and cook the other side for an additional 1 to 2 minutes. You will probably need to lower the heat for the next pancake. Repeat the process until you have used up all of the batter, and keep the pancakes hot in the oven at 200 degrees. Serve.

MAKES 2-3 SERVINGS

Oatmeal

MATERIALS
1 spoon
1 bowl
1 cup

INGREDIENTS
¼ cup dried craisins
1 teaspoon cinnamon
1 tablespoon sugar/1 package of Splenda
¼ cup milk

1/3 cup fresh banana, strawberry or blueberries (optional)
½ cup oatmeal
1 cup water

When I was younger, I used to hate oatmeal, so I'm still a little confused when I see the commercial with the little kids licking their bowls of oatmeal in their mom's mini-van on the way to soccer practice. Oatmeal is probably the most disgusting thing to a little kid, but I've definitely developed an appreciation for it. The trick is very simple: load it up with sweet things.

6 minutes

OATMEAL: Follow the directions on the back of oatmeal box and heat up the water and oats in the microwave until cooked. Add ¼ cup of milk and cook additional 15 seconds. Combine the craisins, cinnamon, sugar and fresh fruit and serve immediately.

MAKES 1 SERVING

Eggs

MATERIALS
A nonstick pan or baking dish
Spatula
Microwave and microwavable plate
Paper towels

One cereal bowl

INGREDIENTS
4 eggs
1 tablespoon of butter
Pam

4 strips of bacon
1 tablespoon sweet basil dried or fresh (chopped finely)
Salt and pepper

In a way, eggs are a very personal food item because everyone makes them differently. Some chefs believe that properly cooked eggs should take about 10-15 minutes on low heat because the high temperature affects the proteins inside the eggs, but you can expedite the process if you do cook your eggs on high heat: just remember the saying "cooked in the pan, overcooked on the plate." Here are some suggestions on how to cook eggs your own way.

5 minutes

TIPS FOR SCRAMBLED EGGS: Use butter. One tablespoon will do. (Butter is the secret to French cooking). When adding it into the pan, make sure the heat is on medium, otherwise the butter will burn and your eggs will be brown.

SCRAMBLED EGGS: On medium heat, add 1 tablespoon of butter and spread it around in the pan until it melts. Add the eggs and continue to stir. Season with salt and pepper. Cook for 2-4 minutes, depending on desired doneness, stirring continually until the eggs have combined together. Serve.

IMPRESS: Add ¼ cup of sour cream before you whisk the eggs.

BAKED EGGS: Preheat the oven to 350 degrees.

Place four strips of bacon on a microwavable plate and cook for approximately 4 minutes, or as directed on package, until the bacon is brown and crispy. When completed, allow the pieces to cool for several minutes, and then crumble them into pieces with your fingers.

On medium heat, melt one tablespoon of butter in a pan (it will take less than one minute).

Turn off the heat. You can also spray it with cooking spray to prevent the eggs from sticking. Crack the eggs into the cereal bowl, trying not to break the yolks. Season with salt and pepper as desired. Pour the eggs into pan and place them in the oven. The eggs should cook very quickly, approximately 5-7 minutes. The whites should be solid white and the yolks should be firm but still bright yellow. Remove the eggs from oven and top with bacon and basil. Serve immediately.

MAKES 4 SERVINGS

TRY: If your measuring cups are made of stainless steel, you can use them on the stove. Use the 1 cup measuring cup and you can use it to fry an egg. On medium heat, just melt a dab of butter, crack in an egg, season it with salt and pepper and cook for 1-2 minutes until it is firm.

TIPS: Don't have basil? Use 1 teaspoon of rosemary instead. No oven? This can be made stovetop-simply place a lid on eggs while they cook.

IMPRESS: Add garlic and top with thinly sliced scallions. Serve with crusty bread, like ciabatta or French baguette.

DON'T: Add onions, because they won't cook in time.

Diner Style Potatoes with Bacon and Caramelized Onions

MATERIALS
A non stick pan or stovetop griddle
Cutting board
Chef's knife
microwavable plate
Spatula

INGREDIENTS
4 pounds potatoes (you can use whatever you have, but look for Yukon gold, russet or even sweet potato)
1 tablespoon butter
1 tablespoon vegetable oil, with an additional 1 tablespoon oil if needed
4 slices of bacon, diced
1 medium size white onion, sliced thinly
Salt and pepper
2 tablespoons rosemary

Potatoes are the staple for a lot of breakfast items, and growing up in Miami, I became accustomed to eating French fries in addition to hash browns for breakfast. These potatoes are very easy to make and can be made in advance and simply reheated in a pan before serving (which is something many diners do).

20 minutes

POTATOES: Wash the potatoes and place them in the microwave. Cook for about 12 minutes or until they're soft but not falling apart.

While the potatoes are in the microwave, combine butter and oil on medium high heat until melted. Add the diced bacon and onions and cook for 10 minutes, stirring often. Season with salt and pepper. You should continue to stir the onions because they tend to stick to the bottom of pan. Once finished, the onions should be soft and the color of caramel or amber. If they start to char or stick to bottom of pan, add one more tablespoon of olive oil and lower the heat slightly, but continue to cook.

Once the bacon is brown and crispy and the onions are soft and golden, discard the extra oil from the pan, leaving about 2 tablespoons of oil. While the bacon and onions are cooking, remove the potatoes from the microwave and chop them into large one inch cubes. Add the potatoes to the onions and bacon and allow to brown (about 5 minutes) so that they develop some color. Season with rosemary. Do not shuffle the potatoes; simply allow them to remain where the fall. Repeat process until all sides of the potatoes are golden brown (5-6 minutes). Taste and season if necessary. Serve when needed.

MAKES 4 LARGE SERVING

IMPRESS: Garnish with fresh parsley and grated parmesan cheese.

REALLY IMPRESS: Sauté 2 cloves of garlic with onions, and drizzle on truffle oil before serving.

TIPS: If you decide to cook with sweet potato, season with 1 teaspoon of nutmeg and 1 tablespoon of cinnamon. Garnish with roughly chopped pecans.

DON'T: Discard hot oil in sink because it will clog the drain. Simply place the oil in an old glass cup or bottle until it cools down to room temperature, and then discard into the garbage.

EVOLUTION: Tortilla with Potato, Spinach and Ham.

Tortilla with Potato, Spinach and Ham

MATERIALS
A non stick pan
Chef's knife
Cutting board
Cereal bowl
Fork
Clean kitchen towel

INGREDIENTS
6 eggs, scrambled
1 package frozen spinach, drained and chopped
4 oz diced maple glazed ham
8 oz of diner Style Potatoes from above (it really doesn't matter how much you have left)
Cooking spray
Salt, pepper
2 tablespoon rosemary (optional)

When I first started having friends over for breakfast after morning practice, I would make pancakes or omelets. This was a very time consuming idea that resulted in everyone eating at different times.

It was my Cuban uncle who first introduced me to the tortilla (aka frittata), which is a Spanish breakfast item that is cooked in a large skillet and filled with whatever you want. This differs from the Mexican tortilla, which is like a soft taco shell. The benefit of making a tortilla is that it only needs a certain time to cook and can serve very large groups. It is also extremely filling and can be made with whatever you want.

40 minutes

TORTILLA: Preheat the oven to 350 degrees. Thaw out the spinach in the microwave according to weight and defrost settings (about 7 minutes). Allow it to cool before ringing out the excess liquid into the sink with the kitchen towel. (*The kitchen towel may seem excessive, but you will need a lot of paper towels for the same job*).

Meanwhile, dice the ham into small pieces (about ¼ inch thick or however you like). In a cereal bowl, crack the eggs. Scramble for 1 minute until combined. Liberally spray the entire pan and add the leftover potatoes, spinach and ham and combine everything so that it is evenly spread out. Season with salt and pepper as needed.

Pour eggs onto the entire mixture and place the pan into the oven. Cook for about 30 minutes, or until frittata is completely set. The top should be slightly golden brown and the interior should be tender. The mixture should not move if you shake the pan. Allow it to cool slightly for about 10 minutes and serve it in the pan at any temperature.

MAKES 6 GIANT SERVINGS

TIPS: Consider adding fresh basil or flat leaf parsley to eggs. Also, check the bottom of pan to make sure that it is oven safe. Be cautious if it has plastic handles.

IMPRESS: Add fresh shrimp to the mixture instead of ham and top with favorite cheese before placing in oven. Serve with roasted asparagus (pg 140).

DON'T: Add more than three different things into mixture, especially not beef, chicken or pork. That's just going to taste strange for breakfast. If you want meat, use ham or cooked sausage.

One Eyed Sandwich

MATERIALS
A non stick pan
Spatula
Cutting board/plate
Small knife

INGREDIENTS
1 egg
1 slice of favorite sandwich bread
Salt and pepper
1 teaspoon butter or cooking spray

I learned this recipe from my grandmother, who used to make it for me ever since I was young. In case it looks familiar, it was also featured in the movie V for Vendetta, when Natalie Portman escapes to her boss' house and first suspects him of being the terrorist, V. The preparation is very simple and this can be made daily and eaten like finger food.

6 minutes

THE SANDWICH: Melt butter in a pan on medium high heat and spray with cooking spray. Meanwhile, cut a circular hole in the middle of the piece of bread, about 1-2 inches in diameter.

When the butter is just starting to sizzle, place the bread in the pan. Carefully break an egg into the open circle in the middle of the bread, trying not to break the yolk. Season with salt and pepper. Cook the egg for about 2-3 minutes (2 minutes will have runnier yolks, 3 minutes will have much firmer yolks). Be careful not to move the bread around, or the yolk will break. After 2-3 minutes, flip the bread. *It should be a dark, golden brown in color, and the egg white should have cooked on the underside of the toast.* Cook until eggs are at desired texture (runnier eggs should need only a minute more).

MAKES 1 SERVING

NOTE: Eggs should achieve the texture of a sunny side up egg, and should take about the equal length of time to cook for desired firmness.

George Foreman French Toast

MATERIALS
George Foreman
Cereal bowl
Fork
Cooking tongs

INGREDIENTS
1 loaf ciabatta bread, about 12 inches long, ends removed and sliced lengthwise into one inch thick pieces
2 tablespoons sugar
1 tablespoon cinnamon
1 teaspoon salt
2 eggs
½ cup milk
1 teaspoon vanilla extract (optional)
Cooking spray

Besides grilling, the George Foreman makes a great sandwich press. I've been making sandwiches on it for a long time, so French toast seemed like the next best thing. When finished, you'll end up with fantastically sweet, crispy bread, which you can eat in your hand, topped with maple syrup, or dipped into our homemade Nutella chocolate sauce.

15 minutes (3 minutes for soaking).

FRENCH TOAST: Heat up the George Foreman on high heat. Crack an egg into the cereal bowl and whisk, then add milk and vanilla. Place the bread slices into the bowl and allow it to soak up the mixture for about 3 minutes. Bread should be soft but not falling apart.

Spray the George Foreman and place the bread on the grill. Season with cinnamon and sugar so that everything is covered and cook for about 5 minutes. Season it again with sugar and cinnamon and turn off the heat. The outside of the French toast should be a nice dark brown because the heat from the griddle would have cooked both the sugar and the cinnamon.

Allow the bread to continue to sit in the grill until it is toasted and crunchy on the outside, but still slightly soft on the inside. Use the time to assemble the filling if you want. Pull out the bread after 2 minutes.

MAKES 4 SERVINGS

IMPRESS: Top with strawberries and peanut butter, or Nutella and bananas, or any combination of the two.

NO GRILL? Use a pan. Heat the pan to medium high heat and add one tablespoon of butter. When butter is melted, add the French toast. Cook for approximately 3-5 minutes or until the French toast is golden brown and crunchy. Flip and cook for an additional 2-3 minutes.

Nutella Sauce

MATERIALS
One cereal bowl
Spoon

INGREDIENTS
½ to 2/3 cup Nutella

Splash of milk (to thin) about 2-3 tablespoons

Nutella is one of the best things on earth. Period. It is a chocolate hazelnut spread prominent in Italy and France, and I have very fond memories of stealing excessive amounts of it (with Crystal, Tulio and Ashley) from the breakfast buffets in one of the hotels we were staying at during a family vacation. In case you haven't had it before, it's great on anything, from crepes to bread, and it's the filling for a lot of chocolates like Ferrero Rocher and Bacio Perugina.

2 minutes

NUTELLA SAUCE: As the bread is cooking, place the Nutella and a splash of milk in cereal bowl. Stir to combine the milk with the spread, and place it in the microwave for 30 seconds. The idea is to make the Nutella mixture the consistency of a sauce, so if necessary add more milk. This recipe should be made at the last minute and the Nutella sauce should be served warm because it will only obtain the desired consistency when heated.

Right before ready to serve, heat it up in the microwave for additional 30 seconds or until it is warm and looks like a chocolate sauce.

TRY: Dip the French toast into a chocolate-coffee drink. For an extravagant breakfast, serve with whipped cream or vanilla ice cream.

IMPRESS: Make sandwiches with two pieces of bread- simply smear a teaspoon of Nutella on each piece and stick them together. Cover them with whipped cream and serve with fresh berries.

Bacon and Tomato Hash

MATERIALS
A non stick pan
1 cutting board
Chef's knife
Wooden spoon
1 microwavable cup

INGREDIENTS
2 vine ripe medium
or large tomato
Four slices of bacon,
diced
Olive oil

1 teaspoon of pinch
of basil
1 teaspoon pinch of
garlic powder
Salt and pepper

Most Americans typically don't eat tomatoes for breakfast, which is more common in the UK, but when combined with bacon, this sweet and salty combination creates an irresistible side dish that is perfect alongside eggs. Impress someone and use this hash as the filling for omelets.

8 minutes

TO COOK: Heat the pan on medium high heat and add oil. Dice the bacon into large pieces, about ½ an inch thick and add it to pan. Because bacon has a high percentage of fat, it will shrink in size, and the amount of fat in the pan will increase. Season with pepper and cook until crispy, stirring often, for about 5 minutes.

Carefully drain the excess fat from the pan and discard it into a glass or the garbage. You should be left with about 1 to 2 tablespoons of oil in the pan, along with the crispy bacon.

The heat should still be on medium high. Your pan may be smoking slightly, but don't worry about it because it will go away once you add the tomatoes. Add the tomatoes and stir. Season with salt, pepper and basil and taste. Combine the tomatoes with the crispy bacon, and cook just until the tomatoes are heated through and their skins are slightly wilting, about 2 minutes. Serve hot.

MAKES 2 SERVING

Tostada de Pan

MATERIALS
George Foreman
Cutting board
Chef's knife
Regular knife

INGREDIENTS
1 loaf of bread (Cuban or Puerto Rican)

Several tablespoons of butter (at room temperature)
Cooking spray

Almost every other morning since I was twelve, I would have swimming practice from about 4:45 to 6:30 am. I had a rough childhood. Luckily our school was close by, so my friends and I had enough time to sit down for breakfast, and one of our usual spots was a Cuban restaurant across from my school called In and Out.

The *desayuno especial*, or breakfast special, was two eggs, fried or scrambled, with ham, Cuban bread and large *café con leche* for a little over three dollars. This method of cooking Cuban bread, or pan cubano, is to lather it with butter and put it in a sandwich press, but the George Foreman yields a very similar results. If you can't find Cuban bread, try Puerto Rican bread or a French baguette.

5 minutes

TOAST BREAD: Heat up the George Foreman and spray with cooking spray. Using the knife and cutting board, slice the bread in half, lengthwise. Using a regular knife, spread butter onto the bread so that it covers the entire surface. (Room temperature butter is really easy to spread). Place bread on the grill and cook until the bread is crispy and the butter is melted, about 2-3 minutes. Serve hot.

MAKES 4 SERVINGS

TRY: This bread is best dipped in café con leche, which is Cuban coffee with milk. It is also known as café au lait (see pg. 40).

IMPRESS: Fill the bread with thin slices of Swiss cheese and sweet ham for a great breakfast sandwich or snack.

Ham and Rice

MATERIALS
1 nonstick pan
1 cutting board
1 knife
1 wooden spoon

INGREDIENTS
2 cup of thick ham, diced in 1 cm long cubes (I use Plumrose)

2 cups of cooked white rice (leftover is best)
2 eggs
¼ cup vegetable oil

In the Philippines, where my mother is from, rice is eaten at all times of the day (seriously, they need to cut that out). As a result, my sister and I grew up (occasionally) eating rice for breakfast. Ham and rice is a great way to use up leftover rice from the previous night and it is truly fried rice for breakfast. Think this is weird? Go to Jolibee, the Filipino McDonalds, if you live in California, where you can eat fried chicken and rice for breakfast.

8 minutes

TO COMBINE: Heat oil on medium high heat and add the ham. Sauté it for about three minutes, until the exteriors are slightly charred but the ham itself is still soft. Add the rice to the pan, and with the back of the spoon, break it up into little pieces so it isn't one large piece. Evenly stir until the rice is full combined with the ham.

TO ADD THE EGGS: Push the ham and rice to one side of the pan, making a small pocket with direct access to the bottom of the pan. Crack the eggs into the pan. Immediately, they should start sizzling. Using the wooden spoon, scramble the eggs together for 30 seconds, until the whites turn translucent. Slowly, combine it with the ham and rice. Don't season. Serve hot.

MAKES 4 SERVINGS

TRY: If you aren't in a rush, allow the rice to sit in the pan on medium high heat for 2-3 minutes afterwards without stirring. It will become very crunchy and form a crispy layer on the bottom.

Bacon and Eggs Pasta Carbonara

MATERIALS
A nonstick pan
Pot
Strainer
Spatula
Wooden spoon
Microwavable plate

Paper towels

INGREDIENTS
1/2 pound of spaghetti or linguini
¼ cup of parmesan cheese

2 eggs
3 slices of bacon
1 tablespoon butter
Cooking spray
Salt and pepper

After hurricane Katrina hit Miami, we experienced a two week blackout. And relying only an ancient charcoal grill that could barely toast a marshmallow, I thought, naturally, why not make pasta? So in between cleaning our driveway and opening the shutters, I spent most of my free time standing over our grill, trying to beg the water to boil.

Try this dish when you are really hungry for breakfast, or the morning after a really fun night.

20 minutes

THE PASTA: Fill a pot with water and bring it to a boil. Meanwhile, place some paper towels on microwavable plate and place the bacon strips on top. Cook them in the microwave for 3 minutes, or until bacon is brown and crispy.

Allow it to cool inside the microwave.

Once the water is boiling, salt the water and add the pasta to the pan. Cook until it is al dente (about 10 minutes) and then drain. Add the drained pasta back to the pot, and using your fingers, crunch up the pieces of bacon and add them to the pot. Mix in cheese, and stir until combined.

FRY THE EGGS: Heat 1 tablespoon in butter on medium heat. Crack two eggs into the pan, making sure not to break the yolks. Cook for 2 minutes, season with salt and pepper, and flip. The whites should be completely white and yolk should still be liquid. Carefully, place the pasta in a serving dish and top with a fried egg. Break the yolk up before serving and toss the pasta at the table. Serve hot.

MAKES 2 LARGE SERVINGS

IMPRESS: The dish is really fantastic with lightly browned garlic (but I don't know if you want to eat that for breakfast). Cook it before you make the eggs, and toss the garlic into pasta with the bacon and cheese.

EVOLUTION: Combine leftovers with a béchamel sauce (pg. 148) until coated and cover with cheese for a creamy baked pasta. Broil everything in the oven until the cheese is bubbly and brown, about 5-8 minutes. Allow it to cool for five minutes before serving.

BREAKFAST DRINKS

Cuban Coffee

MATERIALS
A 3-cup (taza) cafetera
Spoon

INGREDIENTS
3 tablespoons of Cuban Coffee
2 tablespoon of sugar (use only regular sugar)
½ cup of water
Milk to taste

A *cafetera* (ka-fe-Te-ra) is a Spanish or Italian coffee maker that is one of the best inventions ever made. They are widely available and cost about $5-6 for a three (espresso-size) cup maker.

The coffee is also much stronger than regular American coffee so three cups in the morning is enough keep you wired for about twelve hours. (Seriously, if you eye starts to twitch uncontrollably, temporarily switch to tea).

Less than 5 minutes

NOTE:A cafetera comes in three parts: the bottom that holds the water, the metal filter that holds the coffee, and the top where the coffee is dispensed from.

ASSEMBLE: Find the bottom part of the cafetera that holds the water and locate the little screw about ¾ of the way up from the base. This is your water line. You want to fill the container up with water until you reach the screw, (about ½ cup of water).

Next, fill the metal filter with ground Cuban or Italian coffee (most probably the beans will be from Columbia). Make sure you fill it all the way up and pack it down with a spoon so that you have a nicely compacted, flat layer of coffee. Place the coffee filter into the water container- it should fit perfectly. Then screw on the cover and place the cafetera onto the stove on high heat.

BREW: Turn the stove on high. It takes less than 5 minutes to make the coffee. When it is done, there should be steam emitting from the spout of the cafetera, and the brewed coffee should have boiled into the top part of the cafetera.

FOAM: Serve it Cuban style: Use about 2-3 heaping tablespoons of sugar and add 1/2 teaspoon of freshly brewed coffee. Mix it up in a mug with a spoon to dissolve sugar. Pour the entire contents of the cafetera into the cup, stir it up and serve into small espresso cups (or whatever you have).

MAKES 2-3 SERVINGS

A *café con leche or café au lait* is equal parts coffee with steamed milk. Make it *clarito* (lightened, meaning more milk than coffee) or *obscuro* (dark, more coffee than milk).

If one eye begins to twitch uncontrollably, you don't have a vitamin deficiency. It means you are drinking too much coffee.

Left: Metal filter. Center: Holds the water. Right: Coffee dispenser.

Orange Strawberry Smoothie

MATERIALS
1 blender
1 kitchen knife

INGREDIENTS
One cup orange juice
4 ripe strawberries
One 6oz cup of blackberry yogurt
Half a banana, roughly chopped
One 16 oz cup of crushed ice

In case you either had a rough night or just woke up and can't stomach food, smoothies are great for breakfast. Best of all, if you did have a rough night, these recipes can be combined with other liquids (and liquid-gels) that may help you get through that morning class.

4 minutes

BLEND: Cut the ends off of the strawberries and cut them in half. Add them along with the chopped banana, orange juice and yogurt. Blend until smooth. Slowly add crushed ice until it's thick and smooth. Serve.

MAKES 2 SERVINGS

TRY: Substitute pineapple or mango yogurt for a tropical smoothie. For a sweeter option, try orange-tangerine juice instead.

Pineapple and Coconut Smoothie

MATERIALS
1 blender
spoon

INGREDIENTS
1 can chopped pineapple, with juice
½ cup coconut milk
One 6 oz mango yogurt
1 pinch of salt
24 oz of crushed ice

I recreated this smoothie recipe from a drink offered at one of my favorite lunch spots in Miami, so you can thank me for saving you $3.89 plus tax. The original recipe is made with fresh fruit but because mangoes are seasonal, I substituted yogurt so that this drink could be made year round.

4 minutes

ASSEMBLE: Combine all the ingredients into a blender and puree on high until smooth.

Slowly add ice until the smoothie is thick. Serve.

MAKES 2 SERVINGS

TRY: Make this at night: Add ¼ cup pina colada mix and with 2-3 oz of rum (*but only if you're of legal age, or have someone else who can be held liable in the event of disorderly conduct*).

Frozen Coffee

MATERIALS
1 blender

INGREDIENTS
1/2 cup brewed Cuban coffee
¾ cup of milk (stronger) to 1 cup of milk (weaker)

4 tablespoons regular sugar or 1
1 cup crushed ice

Coffee chains like Starbucks and Dunkin Donuts make millions of dollars selling these drinks, so much that fast food restaurants are trying to get in on the action. Because of their relative affordability, many people are addicted to coffee. For me at least, a lot of my attention, especially in morning classes, is dependent on coffee. The trick is to use very strong Cuban coffee (Pilon or Café Bustelo) and for optimum taste, use cream instead of milk.

12 minutes (10 min chilling)

ASSEMBLE: Brew your regular **Cuban** morning coffee. While the coffee is still hot, add the sugar so it can dissolve in the heat. Place the coffee in a mug or bowl and set in the freezer to chill for 10 minutes.
BLEND: Combine chilled ice coffee and milk. Slowly add the crushed ice and blend until smooth and creamy, about 1 minute.

TRY: Adding 1/3 cup of chocolate syrup to brewed coffee. In this case, use milk instead of cream to combine.

IMPRESS: Add 1/3 cup of nutella sauce (pg. 32) to coffee. Serve with whipped cream and chocolate sauce drizzled on top.

MAKES 4 SERVINGS

Poor Man's Tea

MATERIALS
1 mug
1 spoon
1 coffee filter

INGREDIENTS
½ teaspoon dried rosemary
½ teaspoon dried basil

1 teaspoon craisins (about 6)
2 slices of lemon
Sugar to taste

I created this tea when I wanted to drink after dinner that wouldn't keep me up all night.

I know everyone doesn't have a tea ball (which you can buy at some stores for $5 at William Sonoma), so here's an easy solution. Next time you go to the grocery store, buy coffee filters (or a tea ball). When you want tea, fill the coffee filter with the spices and lemon, and then twist the top so that it closes completely. Tie the ends with a piece of floss[1], and you've made a makeshift tea bag.

4 minutes

HEAT: Fill the mug with water and place it in the microwave for 2 minutes.
COMBINE: All the ingredients and one slice of lemon in the tea bag.

SEEP: Add the tea bag to the mug and allow it to seep for about 5 minutes. Add sugar and slice of lemon to taste. Drink.

[1] The effects of combining floss with your tea haven't been scientifically studied, so by making this recipe as suggested, you agree to indemnify Patrick C. Arenson, NewtonLocke, LLC and/or all other affiliated parties stated and unstated for any present or future claims.

SALADS

BUYING FRUITS AND VEGETABLES

The key to saving money is to buy things that are **in season**. Bring this book with you next time you go to the grocery store so you know where you can save the most money.

Selecting great ingredients is easy. For fruits, smell them and touch them. They should always be firm and smell strongly of what they are. *Also try to remember when you are planning on using them:* for later in the week, buy things that are just shy of ripeness. For vegetables, look at the skin and stems. They should feel firm and not be discolored or browning.

Most markets don't have very many options when it comes to salad greens. The basics include **romaine lettuce**, **iceberg lettuce** and occasionally **butter** and **Boston lettuce**. I prefer using romaine lettuce because it is inexpensive, available everywhere, and has a vibrant green color. Try to choose a lettuce that isn't wilting and those that don't have any discoloration on the outer leaves. The stems should also be white.

Also look out for **endive**, **radicchio**, **watercress** and **arugula**. They are more bitter than the regular lettuces, so pair them with a lemon or honey-balsamic vinaigrette (pg. 56-57)

Vegetable	Peak Season	Availability	Preparation	Serve
Artichokes	Spring	Canned (fresh artichokes are seasonal and expensive)	If fresh, trim off rough exterior, so you are left with the heart	If fresh, fried. Otherwise, sautéed, in dips or soups
Asparagus	Summer	Year Round	Snap at ends, line them up and cut	Cooked (roasted, blanched, steamed)
Beans	Varies	Canned	Buy canned if available; except for baked beans, drain of liquid and rinse in water (they are salty)	Add white beans to stews and soups; serve the rest as side warmed through
Broccoli	Winter	Year Round	Take off stems, chop into bite size pieces	Cooked (steamed, sautéed, blanched) Best roasted.
Carrots	Winter	Year Round	Peeled	Any
Cauliflower	Fall and Winter	Year Round	Take off stems, chop into bite sized pieces	Cooked (steamed, blanched) Best roasted
Corn	Summer	Year Round, buy frozen	Remove the husk and wash if fresh	Roasted, sautéed, grilled
Cucumber	Summer	Year Round	Peeled and deseeded (optional)	Raw

Eggplant	Summer and Fall	Year Round	Buy fresh, trim off ends. Remove skin if desired	Sautéed, fried or roasted
Mushrooms	Varies by species	Year Round	Cleaned with moist paper towel (do not soak in water)	Best cooked (sautéed, grilled, roasted)
Onions	N/A	Year Round	Remove outer layer	Any
Peas	Spring	Frozen	Buy frozen	Cooked (microwave)
Potatoes	Varies	Year Round	Any	Any
Squash, pumpkin	Fall and Winter	Fall and Winter	Skinned and deseeded	Roasted
String beans	Varies	Year Round	Remove ends	Blanched or sautéed
Sweet Potatoes	Fall and Winter	Year Round	Skinned	Any
Tomatoes	Spring and Summer	Year Round	Any	Any
Zucchini	Summer	Year Round	Remove ends	Sautéed

Fruits	Peak Season	Availability	Serve	Ideal Appearance	Store in Freezer?
Apples	Fall	Year Round	Eat raw, or sautéed	Skin should be firm and vibrant in color	No
Apricots	Spring and Summer	Spring and Summer (depends)	Grilled	Slightly soft and smell slightly of apricot	No
Avocado	Late Summer and Fall	Mostly Summer (only buy in season)	Raw and seasoned	Soft and bright green	No, go to a Mexican restaurant
Bananas	Year Round	Year Round	Raw, sautéed with brown sugar and butter, or fried	Yellow, not be bruised	Not unless you're making banana bread soon
Blackberries	Summer	Year Round (only buy in season)	As they are	Dark color, soft, intact	Yes, for smoothies
Blueberries	Late Summer	Year Round (only buy in season)	As they are	Firm, sweet and dark blue	Yes, for smoothies
Cherries	Summer and Fall	Year Round (only buy in season)	As they are	Slightly soft	No
Coconut	Depends on location	Depends on location	Juiced; flakes or milk	Should hear a swishing of liquid	No
Fruits	Peak Season	Availability	Serve	Ideal Appearance	Store in Freezer?
Cranberries	Fall and Winter	Buy frozen	Make a jam; very bitter raw.	Red and firm	Yes

Fruits	Peak Season	Availability	Serve	Ideal Appearance	Store in Freezer?
Figs	Summer and Fall	Summer and Fall	Grilled, sautéed, caramelized, reduced	Slightly soft	No
Grapefruits	Varies on variety	Mostly year round	As they are, with some sugar	Firm and smell of grapefruit	No, use juice
Grapes	Late Summer	Year Round	As they are	Firm and pop in mouth	Yes but not permanently stored
Kiwis	Winter and Spring	Winter-Summer	As they are	Brown exterior, firm	No
Lemons	Year Round	Year Round	In dressings, marinades, drinks, teas	Bright yellow, firm flesh	No need
Limes	Summer	Year Round	In drinks, marinades	Smell like lime, bright green	No need
Mango	Late Summer	Mostly Summer	As they are	At optimum, should smell strongly of mango and be soft.	Yes, remove the flesh and freeze.
Oranges	Varies	Mostly Year Round	Segmented or juice	Smell it	No
Fruits	**Peak Season**	**Availability**	**Serve**	**Ideal Appearance**	**Store in Freezer?**
Peaches/Nectarines	Summer	Summer, Fall	Roasted, in crumbles, grilled	Smell like peach, shouldn't be bruised	No
Pears	Varies	Year Round (different varieties)	Roasted, poached, as they are	Skin shouldn't be bruised, smell	No

Pineapples	Summer	Spring, Summer	Grilled	Smell strongly of pineapple, and firm	No, buy canned
Plums	Summer and Fall	Summer, Fall	Grilled	Firm, and vibrant color	No
Raspberries	Summer	Year Round	As they are	Bright red	No
Strawberries	Spring and Summer	Year Round	Sliced with sugar and balsamic vinegar, covered in chocolate	Blood red and firm	Yes, for smoothies and sorbets
Watermelon	Summer	Usually Summer to Autumn	Eat at room temperature	Firm, green exterior, bright red inside	No

Caesar Salad

MATERIALS
1 large, clean jar with lid
1 cutting board
1 knife
1 fork

Dressing

INGREDIENTS
2 egg yolks
2 lemons, juiced
2 tablespoons Dijon mustard
1 large clove garlic, finely chopped
3 tablespoons balsamic vinegar
1 cup olive oil
½ cup parmesan cheese, finely grated
Salt and Pepper

Salad

MATERIALS
Cutting board
Knife
Large bowl

INGREDIENTS
1 large head of romaine lettuce
2 cups croutons, or leftover crusty bread like ciabatta or a French baguette
½ cup parmesan cheese
¾ cup of Caesar salad dressing
1 vine ripe tomato (optional)

Caesar salad is the classic steakhouse salad, and this salad is great alongside hearty entrees like burgers and ribs. Although Caesar dressing is available in all groceries stores, this is a much lighter and healthier dressing, and takes almost no time to make. Classic Caesar salad is made with anchovies, but because people have very distinct opinions about anchovies, I'm not including it in the basic recipe.

One of the easiest methods to making dressing and vinaigrettes is to use old, clean glass jars. Simply place all the ingredients in the jar and shake it when you're ready to serve.

5 minutes

FOR THE DRESSING: Finely chop the garlic into small pieces and place it inside a jar. Throw the lemons into the microwave for 15 seconds, which will make them easier to juice. While making sure to omit the seeds, juice the lemons with the fork into the jar.

Using your hands, separate the egg yolks from the egg whites, catching the yolks in your fingers. Save the whites in bowl and place in the fridge so you can use them later, otherwise discard them into the sink or garbage. Add the yolks and the rest of the ingredients to the jar. When you're ready to serve, simply shake the jar until the dressing is emulsified. Taste and season accordingly.

3 minutes

TO ASSEMBLE THE SALAD: Add a couple tablespoons of dressing to the bottom of the bowl. Cut off the core of the lettuce and discard. Chop the lettuce into bite size pieces and place it into the bowl. Cut the tomatoes into bite size pieces and add them to the bowl, along with the croutons. Top with parmesan cheese. Refrigerate until needed. Right before serving, toss the salad with some dressing so that each leaf is coated.

MAKES 4 SERVINGS

IMPRESS: Microwave several pieces of bacon and add to salad.

REALLY IMPRESS: Using a vegetable peeler, garnish salad with long strands of parmesan cheese.

NOTE: Can't find parmesan cheese? Use Pecorino Romano or Asiago instead.

Balsamic Vinegar

Balsamic vinegar is an extremely versatile ingredient, and can be used in meats, pasta sauces, salads and even desserts. Enjoy it simply as a dipping sauce (olive oil, vinegar and pepper) for warm bread or try it the following ways.

MEATS

For steak, marinate the cuts at room temperature with balsamic vinegar, garlic, salt and pepper an hour before cooking. Broil on high for 3-6 minutes, depending on desired doneness. Flip and allow to brown on the other side. Remove it from oven and let it rest for ten minutes.

For chicken, marinate leg quarters with a couples splashes of balsamic vinegar, the juice of one lemon, rosemary, salt and pepper in a large freezer bag in the refrigerator up to a day before cooking. Roast at 400 degrees for 45 minutes, flipping half way.
For Asian style chicken, marinate with equal parts soy sauce and balsamic vinegar in a large freezer bag.

VINAIGRETTE

For a honey balsamic dressing, add 1-2 tablespoons of honey, to 2/3 cup of balsamic vinegar with 1/3 cup of olive oil. Season with salt and pepper. Shake.

SAUCES

Add balsamic vinegar to your basic tomato sauce for sweetness, or reduce it on medium high heat for five minutes until it develops a syrup-like consistency. Serve with desserts, and even drizzled on steak or roasted shrimp.

DESSERTS

Marinate strawberries in balsamic vinegar and sugar, just until coated. Let it sit for half an hour. Add some fresh fruit like pomegranates (cherries or mulberries?) to the vinegar and mix in equal amounts of chocolate sauce.

Lemon Vinaigrette

MATERIALS
1 jar
1 fork (to juice lemons)
Knife

INGREDIENTS
1/3 cup fresh lemon juice
2/3 cup olive oil
1 tablespoon Dijon mustard (or whatever you have)
1 egg yolk*

Salt and pepper
2 tablespoons honey (preferable, but use can use the same amount of sugar if you don't have honey)

Lemon vinaigrette is a really easy and healthy dressing to master (blah, blah, blah). It can be a marinade for fish and chicken, and as a dressing for couscous. Because lemon is frequently used in Mediterranean cooking, feel free to incorporate it into dishes like freshly grilled vegetables, seafood and taboule.

5 minutes

ASSEMBLE: Place the lemons in the microwave for fifteen seconds to loosen the juices. Squeeze the lemons into the jar with the fork, omitting all seeds. Add the mustard, sugar and season with salt and pepper. Shake it up! You're done.

MAKES 3/4 CUP OF DRESSING

NOTE: I hate mustard but the recipe needs an emulsifier for the dressing to thicken. I know everyone isn't comfortable using yokes yet, so use mustard to replace them.

PS: No jar in sight? I use a water bottle- you can store it in the fridge and keep it until you need it. Just shake it before you use it.

ENTREES

BUYING CHICKEN

Whenever you handle raw chicken, it is extremely important to thoroughly clean every surface that the raw chicken touches. Never chop vegetables on a cutting board that has just touched raw chicken because you risk contaminating your food.

- LEG QUARTERS

This cut combines the thigh and drumstick and is my go-to cut whenever I am roasting chicken. Buy and season them, and you can use them to roast or barbeque (remember if you barbeque chicken, cook it slower, otherwise the outside will char and the inside will remain raw).

- THIGHS

Although I didn't feature any recipes with stewed chicken, thighs retain a lot of moisture and are ideal cooked for a long period of time.

- BREASTS

It is sometimes difficult to find regular chicken breasts, because most people prefer boneless skinless. I recommend boneless skinless because they are cheap and can serve a lot of people, but regular breasts are functional as well: roast them at 400 degrees for 45 minutes with salt and pepper and you're done.

- WINGS

No explanation needed. We are college students after all.

AVOID

- DRUMSTICKS AND WHOLE CHICKENS

Drumsticks tend to dry out very fast and whole chickens are too much work to carve if you don't know what you're doing.

ON SALE

- CHICKEN TENDERLOIN (CHICKEN TENDERS)

Don't buy them unless they are on sale, and if you have a recipe that requires them, simply substitute boneless skinless chicken breasts and no one will know the difference.

STORE

Chicken stores great in the freezer and can be defrosted in the microwave. However, you do not want to keep raw chicken in the fridge for more than 2 days because then it develops a bad smell and will be pretty unappetizing no matter what you try and do to it. (Trust me, I know what chicken smells like after it's been left unrefrigerated for two days).

If you are marinating the chicken, you don't want to marinate the chicken for longer than 1-2 days either, otherwise the acids will begin to cook the chicken.

TEMPERATURE

Cook to an interior temperature of at least 160-165 degrees. The juices will run clear when you cut into it.

Roasted Chicken

MATERIALS
1 Large baking pan
1 pair of kitchen tongs
Aluminum foil

INGREDIENTS
4 chicken leg quarters, washed and patted dry
Cooking spray
Salt and Pepper
1 teaspoon dried Thyme (optional)

If it weren't for fried chicken, roast chicken would top my list as my all time favorite chicken dish.

In France, chefs take *poulet roti* a little too seriously and have even developed an expression to know when the chicken is done cooking: "quand le poulet chante" or "when the chicken sings". (I know these people are crazy!)

Use chicken quarters and this recipe to simplify your life. This is really one of the easiest and best recipes to master.

50 minutes

ROAST: Preheat the oven to 400 degrees. If you have a convection oven, feel free to turn on to the convection roast function. Line the baking pan with aluminum foil, and spray the baking pan with cooking spray.

Remove the chicken from the package and rinse thoroughly with water. Pat it completely dry because the drier it is, the crispier the skin will be. Place the chicken inside the pan and season it liberally with salt, pepper and the teaspoon of thyme. The salt will draw out any excess moisture from the chicken and make it even crispier, so don't omit it.

> Chicken leg quarters are the connected drum stick and thigh pieces. There is no need to bother cutting them into pieces because one quarter is a serving for one person

Roast at 400 degrees for 45 minutes. The chicken should be completely cooked through. Serve immediately.

MAKES 4 SERVINGS

NOTE: There are recipes that suggest adding butter to chicken when roasting it, but it tends to reduce the crispiness of the skin.

IMPRESS: If you are comfortable around the kitchen, try making a quick sauce from the pan drippings. When prepping the baking pan, omit the aluminum foil. After the chicken is done cooking, remove the chicken from the pan and set aside to keep warm. Deglaze the pan with one tablespoon butter and one cup of chicken stock (and half a lemon if you have it). On medium high heat (the pan will still be hot), reduce the sauce while scraping the bottom of the pan for five minutes until it has thickened. Finish with another tablespoon of butter right before serving. Serve the sauce hot with roasted or mashed potatoes.

EVOLUTION: Use leftovers in chicken quesadillas or fried rice.

Chicken Parmesan

MATERIALS
1 nonstick pan
Spatula
Plastic bag
Cereal bowl
Plate lined with paper towels
Cutting board
Chef's knife

INGREDIENTS
2 boneless, skinless chicken breasts
1 cup flour
½ cup of oil
2 tablespoon basil
2 tablespoon oregano
Salt and pepper

6 oz mozzarella cheese

SAUCE
½ cup of tomato sauce, warmed in the microwave (pg. 146, or buy jarred)

If you ever mention chicken parmesan to my Italian teacher, run away! As an Italian woman, she hates being associated with, so she'll probably make a face of disgust. Chicken parmesan, she says, is an Italian-American invention. In Italy, chicken parmesan didn't exist, so don't go looking for it. *Avete capito*?

This dish is perhaps one of the most popular meals amongst college students. To preserve the crispiness of the chicken, heat up the sauce separately in the microwave and simply pour it over before you're ready to serve.

15 minutes

PREP: Using your hand as a guide, split the chicken breast in half lengthwise so that you are left with two pieces of equal size and thickness. (Press gently down on the chicken, and slide your knife carefully across the middle of the chicken). In the plastic bag, combine the flour, basil and oregano and throw in the chicken. Shake until the chicken is completely coated.

FRY: Heat up the oil on medium high heat, and add the chicken after about 2 minutes. Pan fry the chicken for about 4-5 minutes. Flip and continue to cook for an additional 2-3 minutes or until the chicken is completely cooked all the way through. It should be golden brown in color. Place the chicken on the plate lined with paper towels to drain, and discard the excess oil.

FINISH: On broil, place the chicken back in the nonstick pan.

Place the pieces of cheese atop the chicken and finish melting the cheese in the oven for 2-3 minutes. It should be slightly browned on top when finished. Heat up the tomato sauce in the microwave and pour onto the chicken at the last minute. Serve immediately.

IMPRESS: Make a *Chicken Parmesan Involtini*, which basically means chicken stuffed with mozzarella, and rolled like a sleeping bag. Preheat the oven to 350 degrees. Following the same steps: simply split the chicken breast widthwise, making sure to not cut all the way through (the two parts of the breast should be hinged together). Insert a slice of mozzarella or provolone cheese and a fresh basil leaf inside the chicken, and fold the other breast over so that it resembles its original appearance. Secure the stuffing with toothpicks on the loose end. Coat with flour and pan fry as directed. When both sides are golden brown, place the pan in the oven and continue cooking the chicken for an additional 8-10 minutes. Pour the tomato sauce on top before serving.

EVOLUTION: Make a Chicken Parmesan Pizza. Using store bought pizza dough and leftover mozzarella and tomato sauce, simply slice the leftover chicken, top the pizza with remaining condiments and bake at 500 degrees for 10-12 minutes, or until the pizza is browned and crispy.

MAKES 2 SERVING

Chicken Milanese

MATERIALS
A nonstick pan
Chopping board
Chef's knife
Spatula
Cereal bowl
2 plates
Paper towels or old newspaper
Plastic bag (from a grocery store)

INGREDIENTS
2 chicken breasts, sliced
1 cup flour
1 and 1/2 cups cold water, with additional 2 tablespoons
2 cups of panko breadcrumbs
Salt and pepper
2 tablespoons Lemon or lime zest (optional)
1 teaspoon basil
1 teaspoon oregano (optional)
1 cup vegetable oil

Chicken Milanese is known by many different names all over the world. It's *katsu* in Japan, a chicken *cutlet* in the southern US and a *pollo empanizado* in Spanish countries,

The traditional chicken Milanese is made with breadcrumbs and egg wash, but for the crispiest chicken, look for panko breadcrumbs, which are Japanese style bread crumbs. To make the basic breading is a process, but once mastered, it can be applied to a lot of different applications.

20 minutes

PREP: Slice the chicken into long strips and season with salt and pepper on both sides. Set up your assembly station. Mix flour and ice cold water to make tempura batter, and add the zest. On one of the plates, spread out the panko breadcrumbs. Now you are ready to bread.

TO BREAD: Use only one hand to coat so that you are left with one free hand to cook with. Bread the chicken as follows: grab a piece of chicken and coat it in tempura batter until it is completely covered, then dip it into the panko. As you proceed through the steps, make sure to take your time and coat everything.

COOK: Using the tongs, gently place the chicken in the oil. The oil should be sizzling when you add the chicken, but not jumping out at you. If the oil is too hot, remove the pan from heat and bring the temperature lower to about a medium high heat. Repeat the process of breading the chicken and adding it to the pan. (*Keep in mind that the oil will reduce in temperature as you add more chicken to the pan, so you might have to bring the heat back up after you have added the chicken*).

Cook the chicken until golden brown on one side, about 4-5 minutes, then flip and repeat. *Be mindful that the chicken should constantly be at a sizzle, and you might have to readjust the heat as you continue through the recipe.*

Cover the last plate with newspaper or paper towels, and drain the chicken onto it. (If all the chicken does not fit in the pan at once while you were cooking, make two batches, keeping the cooked chicken warm in the oven at 200 degrees). Serve hot or at room temperature the next day.

DISPOSING OF OIL: When you are finished cooking, allow the oil to come room temperature before disposing it. Do not dispose of it into the drain, as it will clog it. Instead, dispose it directly into the garbage.

MAKES 2 SERVINGS

NOTE: When cooking with chicken, one must be careful with maintaining a clean environment. Clean everything that has touched the raw chicken thoroughly with hot water, and dispose of the leftover panko, egg, and flour.

Be careful when heating up the oil and make sure no one is around you. Bring the heat up to medium high heat and let it heat up for 2 minutes. Place your hand 6 inches above the pan. If you can feel the heat, it is ready. If the pan starts to smoke, remove the pan from the heat and let it cool.

Chicken Quesadilla

MATERIALS
2 pans, one covered
with aluminum foil
on the bottom
Spatula
Cutting board
Chef's knife
Microwavable bowl
Tablespoon

INGREDIENTS
6-8 oz chicken*
½ cup of salsa
2 salad wraps, or
thin tortillas
¾ cup of grated
cheddar cheese (or
whatever yellow
cheese you have)
½ cup of canned
black beans, heated
1 tablespoon oil

*Something heavy and
unnecessary*
(Economy size can
of tomato sauce,
calculus book)
1 tablespoon Tabasco
sauce (optional)
Guacamole and sour
cream (optional)
Salt and pepper
Cooking spray

One of the best fish dishes that I have ever eaten was not from Paris, Florence or Madrid, but from Mexico City, so if anyone has anything to say about Mexican food, they have to go through me first.

We college students are the masters of Mexican food, so I don't have to tell you how good or how many things you can do with Mexican food. The leftovers are also great for breakfast the next day.

18 minutes

ASSEMBLE: Open a can of black beans and drain out some of the liquid. Place it in the microwavable bowl and heat up for about 1 to 1 1/2 minutes, or until the contents are hot. Season with pepper (canned beans are usually pretty salty) and hot sauce.

On medium heat, heat oil in pan just to coat the bottom, and spray cooking spray to prevent sticking.

Meanwhile, on a cutting board, lay out one wrap. Using a tablespoon, add a thin layer of black beans to one half of the wrap. Add chicken and grated cheese so that it is restricted to the same half of the wrap. Fold over the other half of the wrap so it resembles a half moon.

Heat up a pan on medium high heat and place the quesadilla into it. Place the second pan (that is covered with foil) on top of the quesadilla. Insert the heavy object inside pan so that it begins to flatten out quesadilla. Be careful not to press too hard, otherwise the contents will end up with pan and will make it hard to clean later.

After 3-4 minutes or until cheese has started to melt and the wrap is slightly brown and crispy, remove the second pan and flip the quesadilla. Repeat the process, cooking the quesadilla until the cheese is completely melted and exterior is slightly crispy. Serve immediately. Use salsa as a dipping sauce, and guacamole and sour cream as a topper.

MAKES 2 SERVINGS

TRY: Add pieces of bacon to the quesadilla.

VEGETARIAN: Substitute shrimp (seasoned with paprika and garlic powder)

Chicken from this recipe can come from several different sources. If you have **leftover chicken Milanese** or **grilled chicken,** they make the perfect fillers. A simply grilled chicken breast seasoned with salt, pepper and adobo seasoning is another great option, but if you have a large group coming over, go to the grocery store and buy a **rotisserie chicken** (which should be about 6 dollars). Remove the skin and discard. Then remove the meat, chop up into bite size pieces and now you have a lot of chicken that will yield approximately 5 quesadillas.

EVOLUTION: Make burritos with leftover mix, Mexican chicken salad, scrambled eggs with black beans and salsa, or simple rice and chicken.

NOTE: You don't necessarily need to cover another pan in aluminum foil. You just want to add some pressure to the quesadilla so it flattens and browns slightly.

Pollo a la Plancha with Mojo Sauce

MATERIALS
Cutting board
Knife
Cereal bowl
Spoon

INGREDIENTS
2 chicken breasts, split in half lengthwise
Adobo seasoning (only if you have it, don't buy it!)
Salt and Pepper
Cooking spray
2 tablespoons oil

MOJO SAUCE
1/3 cup of orange juice
2 limes, juiced
3 cloves of garlic, minced
1 teaspoon parsley (optional)
1/2 cup olive oil

This is comfort Cuban cooking at its best and a perfect dish to eat with white rice and fried bananas called *maduros* along with this easy mojo sauce.

Mojo is a traditional Cuban sauce made from sour oranges, garlic and oil. However, because sour orange juice is hard to find, I use lime juice instead.

15 minutes

PREP: Begin by heating up the George Foreman on high heat and spray with cooking spray. Place the limes in the microwave and heat for 20 seconds so the heat can help release the juice. Remove the limes from microwave and juice them into the bowl.

Meanwhile finely mince the garlic and add it into the same bowl. Season with basil, parsley, salt and pepper and two tablespoons of olive oil.

PREPING THE CHICKEN: Using the same chopping board, split the chicken breast lengthwise so that you have two pieces of equal width. Repeat the process with the other chicken. Season the chicken with salt, pepper and adobo seasoning and be generous with it.

If you have a grill, this would be a great time to use it; just make sure the chicken has some olive oil so it won't stick. Grill or place in a sauté pan with the oil on medium high heat. After 4 minutes, flip the chicken and cook for an additional 2-3 minutes, or until the chicken is completely cooked through. Serve with the mojo sauce.

MAKES 2 SERVINGS

TIPS*: *Maduros* can be purchased in the frozen food section of the grocery stores and made in the microwave.

IMPRESS: Season maduros with equal amounts of cinnamon and sugar before heating.

TRY: Marinate the chicken in the garlic sauce for several hours or overnight for maximum flavor.

EVOLUTION: Cuban Pit-za.

Cuban Pit-za

MATERIALS
1 baking sheet
Cutting board
Chef's knife
Can opener

INGREDIENTS
2 slices of pita bread
4-6 oz of leftover chicken, diced
2 maduros, defrosted in microwave and chopped
1/2 cup of black beans, drained
1/2 cup of frozen corn, defrosted

2 large handfuls of mozzarella cheese (buy an 8 oz package and make extra pitas for later)
Salt and pepper
1 tablespoon oil or cooking spray

Rachel Ray has a huge affinity for combining the names of two completely different dishes, so I'm glad I came up with this contraction before she could. HA!

Pita is one of the best substitutes for pizza dough because it has an extremely long shelf life, crisps up really nicely in the oven and is actually pretty healthy for you.

This recipe will have leftover maduros (they are Cuban plantains available precooked in the frozen section of most grocery stores), corn, cheese and black beans, so try making this for a party and just make a couple more pitzas.

15 minutes

Preheat the oven to as hot as it can go, but at least 450 degrees.

PREP: Microwave the maduros and corn, so that they are both defrosted. Drain the black beans by removing the lid, and using it as a strainer as you pour the excess liquid into the sink. Chop the maduros and chicken into bite size pieces.

ASSEMBLE: Add chicken, corn, black beans and maduros to the pita. Top with cheese and season with salt and pepper.

BAKE: Oil the baking sheet to prevent any sticking, and add

the pitas. Place into the oven for about 5-6 minutes. Remove when the cheese has melted and has started to brown only slightly. If it isn't yet finished, allow to cook for an additional 2 minutes, but make sure to check because the oven will be hot. Serve hot or at room temperature, or give it to your friends who have had too much to drink at any temperature because they won't remember anyways.

YIELDS 4-5 Pit-zas (if you buy a whole package of pita bread)

NO MADUROS? Don't worry about it. Add some thinly sliced carrots instead. It's a pizza, not a chemistry test.

TRY: Try adding store bought salsa as a tomato sauce. Make this for a party!

9 Spice Chicken

MATERIALS
Non stick pan
Kitchen tongs
Aluminum foil

INGREDIENTS
2 boneless, skinless chicken breasts
1 tablespoon olive oil
One teaspoon each of:
Cinnamon
Salt
Pepper
Paprika
Curry powder
Basil
Oregano
Cayenne pepper
Garlic powder
1-2 tablespoons of honey

On Miami Beach, there's a famous restaurant at the Delano Hotel called Blue Door. Because it is on the beach and a hot spot for the rich and famous, they can charge 18 dollars for a piece of cheese on an oversized plate.

One day, I went there for lunch and ordered their chicken with 12 spices and honey, come to find out 25 dollars later that it's a simple mammoth chicken kebab- what a waste! Moral of the story: don't eat where tourists eat, and make that sh*t at home.

20 minutes

Preheat the oven to 350 degrees.

SEASON: Coat the chicken with olive oil. Sprinkle it with equal amounts of each of the seasonings. *It's ok if you don't have all the spices, just use what you have. Make sure the whole breast is covered, but you don't want to make it as thick as a rub.*

GRILL OR OVEN?

GRILL: Add the chicken to a pan on high heat. Sear the chicken for 2 minutes, but check it at 1 ½ minutes just in case (check the picture for an idea). The idea is to get a nice brown coat on the chicken but we aren't cooking it. It should be browned and dark. Flip it and sear for another 1-2 minutes.

OVEN: Place the pan in the oven and bake at 375 degrees for 10-12 minutes. Don't open the oven door. Take it out of the oven and let it sit for about 5 minutes (covered with aluminum foil) before you carve. Drizzle with honey and the heat will help the honey melt. Serve hot or at room temperature.

EVOLUTION: Use this basic chicken recipe and add it to anything you want.

MAKES 2 SERVINGS

Sweet and Sour Chicken

MATERIALS
Non stick pan
Cutting board
Chef's knife
A wooden spoon
Plate lined with
paper towels
Plastic bag
One small bowl/cup

INGREDIENTS
2 boneless, skinless
chicken breasts
2/3 cup of flour (just
to coat)
1 cup of vegetable oil
Salt and pepper

Sweet and Sour Sauce

1 small can of
pineapple, drained
(set aside 2/3 cup of
pineapple juice)
2/3 cup water
1 lemon, juiced
and two pieces of
zest (optional)
3 tablespoons sugar
3 cloves of garlic
(optional)
1 red/orange bell
pepper, sliced
(optional)

Whenever I think of sweet and sour chicken, I usually picture very small pieces of chicken surrounded by a lot of breading. This version utilizes a much simpler approach, with simply fried chicken without any unnecessary filler. For a more classic sweet and sour sauce, feel free to add sliced red and orange bell peppers.

20 minutes

TO PREP: Slice chicken into one inch, bite size pieces and place them inside the plastic bag. *When cooking with raw chicken, make sure to clean the surfaces and the cutting board thoroughly.*

Add the flour to the bag, along with the salt and pepper. Roll the chicken around, until everything is coated.

TO FRY: Preheat the pan to medium high heat. When the pan is hot enough (about 2 minutes), add the chicken. The chicken should sizzle but the oil shouldn't be splashing; if the oil is too hot, then lower the heat, but remember that the heat of the oil will drop as you add more chicken. Fry the chicken for about 3-4 minutes, depending on the thickness.

Flip and continue to cook until the chicken is cooked completely through and golden brown. Repeat as necessary. Drain the chicken on the plate lined with paper towels and keep them warm in the oven. Discard the excess oil.

FOR THE SAUCE: On high heat, add the drained pineapple juice, lemon juice, water and sugar to the same pan. Deglaze the pan by scraping the excess bits of chicken from the bottom. Cook for 5 minutes. After 5 minutes, the chicken should have a syrup-like consistency. Add the chicken back to the sauce, and serve hot with white rice.

NOTE: A secret many Chinese restaurants probably want to keep on the down-low is that their unnaturally orange sweet and sour sauce is just that: *unnatural*. Many restaurants use red or orange food coloring to obtain the color. Because the taste is unaffected by the color, don't be alarmed that this chicken is not the same color that you are used to.

MAKES 2-3 SERVINGS

Honey Garlic Chicken

MATERIALS
Non stick pan
Cutting board
Chef's knife
Kitchen tongs
Plate lined with
paper towels
Plastic bag

INGREDIENTS
2 boneless, skinless
chicken breasts
2/3 cup of flour (just
to coat)
1 cup of vegetable oil
Salt and pepper

HONEY GARLIC SAUCE
8 cloves of garlic, 4
of them minced
2 tablespoons of
honey
¾ cup of water
2 tablespoons brown
sugar

Over Christmas break, my sister and I tried a restaurant called Philippe's on Miami Beach, as an experiment of what upscale Chinese dining could be. We tried four different things, and no matter what it was called on the menu, everything we had was red, extremely sweet and overpriced. The next day, I had a cooking cram session, and I tested all the Asian style chicken recipes for this book. Thanks to my decade long love of take-out Chinese food, we were happy to see that these recipes beat out Philippe's, and best of all, everything was cheap (and not red).

20 minutes

PREP: Slice the chicken into one inch, bite size pieces and place them inside the plastic bag. *When cooking with raw chicken, make sure to clean the surfaces and the cutting board thoroughly.*

Add the flour to the bag, along with the salt and pepper. Roll the chicken around, until everything is coated.

FRY: Preheat the pan to medium high heat. When the pan is hot enough, add the chicken. The chicken should sizzle but the oil shouldn't be splashing; if the oil is too hot, then lower the heat, but remember that the heat of the oil will drop as you add more chicken. Fry the chicken for about 3-4 minutes per side, depending on the thickness and size. Flip and continue to cook until the chicken is cooked completely through and golden brown. Repeat as necessary. Drain the chicken on the plate and keep them warm in the oven. Discard the excess oil.

FOR THE SAUCE: Once you have discarded the excess oil, add the water to the pan. Bring the heat up to high.

Scrape off any of the bits from the bottom of the pan, which will help flavor the sauce. Add the garlic, brown sugar and honey and cook for 5 minutes.

After 5 minutes, the sauce should be thick and syrup like. Add the chicken back to the pan and stir until everything is coated. Serve hot with white rice.

MAKES   2-3   SERVINGS

Orange Chicken

MATERIALS
Non stick pan
Cutting board
Chef's knife
A wooden spoon
Plate lined with
paper towels
Plastic bag

INGREDIENTS
2 boneless, skinless
chicken breast
¾ cup of flour (just
to coat)
1 cup of vegetable oil
Salt and pepper

ORANGE SAUCE
2 tablespoons of soy
sauce
2 tablespoon of sugar
2/3 cup of orange
juice
¼ cup of water
2 teaspoons orange
zest (optional)

I know several people that have a sincere and unhealthy obsession with orange chicken (you know who you are) and a week doesn't go by when I'm not being persuaded into eating it. This is an improved version of the food court staple, except I'm not going to spear you with a toothpick or yell at you as you pass by.

20 minutes

PREP: Slice the chicken into one inch, bite size pieces and place them inside the plastic bag. *When cooking with raw chicken, make sure to clean the surfaces and the cutting board thoroughly.* Add the flour to the bag, along with the salt and pepper. Roll the chicken around until everything is coated.

FRY: Preheat the pan to medium high heat. When the pan is hot enough, add the chicken. The chicken should sizzle but the oil shouldn't be splashing; if the oil is too hot, then lower the heat, but remember that the heat of the oil will drop as you add more chicken. Fry the chicken for about 3-4 minutes, depending on the thickness and size. Flip and continue to cook until the chicken is cooked completely through and golden brown. Repeat as necessary. Drain the chicken on the plate and keep it warm in the oven. Discard excess oil.

FOR THE SAUCE: On medium, high heat, combine the soy sauce, water, sugar and orange juice and zest to the same pan. Deglaze the pan by scraping the excess bits of chicken from the bottom of the pan. Cook on high heat for 5 minutes, until the sauce is slightly thickened. Add the chicken back to the sauce, turn off the heat, and toss until coated. Serve.

MAKES 2 SERVINGS

Soy Glazed Chicken Wings

MATERIALS
Baking sheet
1 bowl
Aluminum foil
Spoon

1 pair kitchen tongs

INGREDIENTS
½ cup soy sauce
¼ cup sugar

Sesame seeds (optional)
1 ½-2 pounds chicken wings

My mother always had a great way of making chicken wings. Her secret, despite what she may say, is guilt, not love, so I'm forced to devour them in obscene quantities in order to stay in her good graces.

The trick is to marinate. Once you get home from the grocery store, separate the wings into plastic bags and pour in the marinade. Place two bags in the freezer for later and keep one in the fridge so that they're ready for you whenever you're hungry.

28 minutes

MARINADE: In the bowl, combine the soy sauce and sugar. Stir until most of the sugar dissolves, about one minute. Add the wings and toss the sauce with the wings so that everything is covered. Cover them with aluminum foil and place in the fridge for up to 2 days, or cook immediately.

ROAST: Preheat the oven to 425 degrees.

Line the baking sheet with aluminum foil. Using the tongs, remove marinated chicken wings from the bowl and allow some of the liquid to drain back into the bowl. Remember, the dryer the wing, the crispier the skin.

Assemble the wings on a single layer on the baking sheet and roast for 15 minutes at 425 degrees. Flip the wings between 10-12 minutes so that both sides become browned. When they are dark golden brown and crispy, remove them from the oven. Place them on a plate and sprinkle with sesame seeds. Serve hot or at room temperature.

BUYING PORK

When I visited the Philippines, I ordered a dish called "crispy pork pata" (fried pork) in one restaurant and unbeknownst to me, it turned out to be my mother's favorite dish. I remember seeing her slowly ascend from her table with a clean plate in hand, as she followed the smell to my table and began picking pieces off of my plate as if I was the buffet line. I had to tell the waiter that this strange, maybe even homeless lady was trying to eat my food and that they should keep a close eye on her. Unfortunately, they didn't understand what I was saying and I ended up leaving that lunch very hungry.

Pork is really a great alternative to beef but because most cuts of pork are inaccessible or require too much time to cook, there is a very limited selection in the store.

BUY

- PORK CHOPS

The thinner pork chops are great if you want to bread and fry them (and are much cheaper as well) but the thick ones are best for browning on the stove and roasting in the oven. Remember *thin, fry, dry*.

- PORK LOIN

Pork loin is a great piece of meat, and I actually prefer it to the tenderloin because there is a large strip of fat on the top of the loin. Please make sure you don't cut it off before you cook it. The fat locks in the moisture of the meat and you end up with a great, tender piece.

ON SALE

- PORK TENDERLOIN

Probably the most expensive cut of pork besides ribs, you will usually find this vacuum packed in an airtight package. Keep in mind that if you don't buy the already seasoned pork tenderloin (which I advise you not to), and then each package will yield two loins.

- BABY BACK RIBS

They can be expensive so if you do buy them for a party, consider serving them as an appetizer. When you buy ribs, do not cut them into smaller portions before cooking. *Ribs are best cooked whole and sliced afterwards.*

AVOID

- SPARE RIBS

This cut of meat is very tough and difficult to work with if it isn't cooked for a long enough time.

- BONELESS PORK CHOP

Pork chops, especially skinnier pork chops, contain most of their moisture closer to the bone. I would skip these altogether as they will very easily to dry out.

STORE

Store in the freezer in a freezer safe bag for several months, or keep in the fridge marinating for about 2-3 days.

Barbecue Ribs

MATERIALS
Baking sheet (or roasting pan if you have one), wrapped in aluminum foil
Tongs
Microwavable bowl
Spoon

INGREDIENTS
For the rub:
5 tablespoons of paprika
1 tablespoon salt
3 tablespoons pepper
2 tablespoons dried basil
2 tablespoons garlic powder
3 tablespoons curry powder

1 large package of ribs (about 2 large slabs)*

Barbecue Sauce
1 cup of favorite barbeque sauce
¼ cup of leftover rub seasoning
2 tablespoons balsamic vinegar
2 tablespoons brown sugar (optional)

Traditionally smoked at about 225 degrees for 4-6 hours ("low and slow"), barbecued ribs are not for everyday dinners. But reserved for a special occasion, these fall-off-the-bone ribs are a tender and juicy entrée that are equally impressive as they are easy to make. Simply make the rub, place them in the oven and walk away.

A rub refers to the seasoning of the meat, and ideally you want a thick coating so that it forms a crust when cooked. There are two basic types of rubs, a *wet rub* and a *dry rub*. These ribs use a dry rub
because it is easier to make and less messy- it also creates a nice crust on the outside.

2 hours

ASSEMBLE: Preheat the oven to 300 degrees. Combine the rub ingredients together and mix. Rub all over the ribs. Don't be shy! Cover so that it coats on both sides.

COOK: Wrap the ribs in aluminum foil. Poke some small holes in the top so that the steam can be released. Place on a baking sheet and cook for 1 and 45 minutes.
Do something else.

SAUCE: After 1 hour and 45 minutes, combine barbeque sauce, leftover rub seasoning, balsamic vinegar and brown sugar in a microwavable bowl. Stir together and heat for about a minute, until everything has dissolved together. Carefully, remove the ribs from the foil. Coat the ribs evenly with the barbeque sauce on all sides. Place it back in the oven for an additional 15 minutes. The brown sugar and balsamic vinegar will cause the ribs to brown a little, but they shouldn't be burned.

The ribs should be about to fall off the bone. If not, cool for an additional 20-30 minutes at the same temperature. Allow the meat to rest for 10 minutes, covered in foil, before serving.

MAKES 2-3 SERVINGS

*Save leftover rib seasoning in a small Tupperware. Use it for chicken or steak that you're cooking on the grill.

TIPS: *Don't listen to your parents if they tell you to boil the ribs to make them tender. The flavor from the ribs will go in the water and they will be dry if you try and cook them because all the fat would have gone into the water too. Also, don't apply barbeque sauce until the end otherwise the sugar in the barbeque sauce will scorch the ribs.*

The weight of the ribs is really not that important, as long as everything has equal access to heat. Two slabs of ribs should be fine.

Pork Loin

MATERIALS
Roasting pan
Spatula
Kitchen tongs
Cutting board
Knife

INGREDIENTS
1 5lb pork loin
Rib rub (see pg. 87)
or equal amounts
salt, pepper and
paprika, basil

2 tablespoons olive
oil
Barbeque   sauce
(optional)

The first time I made a large dinner for my friends, at the request for something different (Tulio cough!) I served marinated pork tenderloin. The end was result was delicious and moist, but I still didn't forget how much I paid for the pork or the attention it demanded.   Aside from being almost twice the price of regular pork loin, pork tenderloin lacks the layer of fat that envelops the top side of pork loin, which means it dries out easily. A large pork loin may cost about $15, but it can easily serve 6 people. It is great simply roasted, and all it really requires is liberal seasoning.

1 hour

TO ROAST: Preheat the oven to 400 degrees.
Rub the pork loin with the rub. Cover it everywhere! Drizzle the bottom of roasting pan with olive oil to prevent sticking. Place the pork loin in the pan.

Roast for 1 hour, but check on it after 50 minutes. The interior temperature should be 160 degrees. But touch it. The meat should be firm. *Basically poke your index finger- that's what it should feel like.*

Allow the meat to rest for ten minutes covered in foil. Slice the meat in relatively thin pieces, about ½ inch thick. The insides should be moist and almost completely white, but if it is still undercooked, place the meat back in the oven for another ten minutes or until the meat is cooked.

MAKES 6 SERVINGS

Pan con Lechon

MATERIALS
Non stick pan
Wooden spoon
George Foreman grill
Chef's Knife
Cutting board

INGREDIENTS
Half a loaf of Cuban (or Puerto Rican) bread
1 medium white or yellow onion
About 8-10 oz of leftover pork loin (just to fill it up)
2 tablespoons olive oil
Salt and pepper

Mojo Sauce
1/3 cup of orange juice (no pulp)
2 limes, juiced
3 clove garlic, minced
1 teaspoon parsley (optional)
1/2 cup olive oil

Whenever friends or relatives visit Miami for the first time, I always try and introduce them to Cuban food because it is such a large part of the Miami culture. For this recipe, use leftover pork (from above) with sautéed onions and a quick mojo sauce.

15 minutes

SAUTE: Because the onions take the longest, sauté them first. Trust me, don't bypass this step. Cut the onion in half lengthwise and thinly slice them so they look like half moons. Add them to the pan on medium high heat. Cook for about 10 minutes, stirring often. The objective is to get the onions a nice deep brown color (aka *caramelizing* the onions).

Season with salt and pepper, and the salt will help expel some of the liquid from the onions.

GRILL: Split the Cuban bread in half and add the pork loin. Place it in the George Foreman and cook until the bread is pressed and crunchy, about 6-8 minutes.

FINISH: Remove the sandwich from the press and open it up. Spoon in the caramelized onions. Add a couple tablespoons of the mojo sauce. Serve hot.

MAKES 3 LARGE SANDWICHES

Medianoche

MATERIALS
George Foreman grill
Chef's Knife
Cutting Board

INGREDIENTS
1 loaf Cuban bread
½ pound of sweet ham
½ pound roast pork
1/3 pound Swiss cheese
Pickles to disperse throughout
sandwich *(optional)
3 tablespoons of mustard (optional)

*Buy the canned pickles that are cut into small, circular discs

The famous Medianoche (also known as Cuban sandwiches) can honestly be appreciated at any time of the day, and because there are many Cuban restaurants open 24/7 in Miami, they literally are. Medianoches are typically made with sweet ham, roast pork, cheese, pickles and sometimes even mustard and mayonnaise, so this is a good way to get rid of some of those leftover cold cuts. You can also find the sandwich being made on a sweet yellow Puerto Rican bread as well as the traditional Cuban bread.

10 minutes

NOTE: I don't like mayonnaise or mustard, so feel free to omit them from the recipe as I will- it's also more traditional to leave out the condiments. However, the pickle is something that you will always find.

ASSEMBLE: Split the bread and half and top the sandwich with the ham, cheese, pork and pickles.

GRILL: Using the George Foreman, grill the sandwich for about 5-7 minutes, until the cheese is almost melted and the bread is pressed.

MAKES 4 GIANT SANDWICHES

BUYING BEEF

Marbling is the key to buying meat and it refers to the lines of fat that run throughout the meat. I know many of you are skittish when the idea of fat is introduced into the conversation, but it is one of the most important parts about buying great meat. For example, the most expensive beef in the world comes from Japan and is known as **Kobe** beef: it is valued because of its intense marbling. It is also expensive as hell! If you go to a restaurant, a little 4 oz piece may cost more than $40. *Cough, Kobe Club!*

The *USDA* has two basic ratings for meat that you should know about. The first is called **choice**, which is what you should expect to find in the grocery store, and the second is **prime**, which you should expect to find at a steak house or a fancy butcher shop. Of course, prime has better marbling, but it is also much more expensive.

BUY

If you are buying for a large group, there is no better place to buy meat than a large discount warehouse store like **Costco.** And even if you're not, you can buy in bulk and freeze separately. However, when you buy at these discount warehouses, the meat isn't portioned or sliced yet, so save some time butchering and ask the guys behind the window to butcher it up for you.

To select meat, first search out the thin white lines of fat that run throughout the meat. Ideally, the best cuts of meat have the most marbling because when the meat is cooked, the fat will keep the meat moist and tender. You don't want the fat to be in large thick segments, and you also want to resist trimming all of the fat off of the steaks because you'll end up with a tough piece of meat. It is also because of this fat content that cuts like beef chuck or beef shoulder are better than a tenderloin or rib eye if you are making a stew.

PS. Never pass up the chance to try Kobe beef on someone else' tab.

- GROUND BEEF

  Ground beef is a great, versatile ingredient that can be transformed into a lot of different things. I generally opt for 80-20 ground beef, which refers to 80% meat and 20% fat (just check the label).

- CHUCK

  Chuck is a great option for stews- just remember to cook the meat slowly (350 degrees in the oven for 2 hours) covered in a braising liquid like red wine and beef stock.

- SKIRT STEAK

  This is probably one of the best pieces of meat to buy, because it combines the optimum level of price and tenderness. In Miami, it is called *churasco*. **When you buy it, make sure the skirt is cut off, because it is very time consuming to do it yourself.** Trust me.

- SIRLOIN

  If you find a thin, boneless sirloin, its great breaded and fried (called *bistec empanizado* in Spanish). The cut of meat is called also known as palomilla.

- SHORT RIBS and BEEF SHANKS

  A good deal for short ribs is about $3-$4 a pound and $2 for beef shanks: cook them at 300 degrees for 2 hours as well. Buy more than you think because they cook down a lot.

- NEW YORK STRIP

The New York Strip is often favored above the tenderloin, rib eye and porterhouse in quality cuts, so they will probably be priced around the same. Buy a thicker piece (about 1 inch) with a lot of marbling.

ON SALE

- PORTERHOUSE

The porterhouse combines half a piece of New York Strip and half a piece of tenderloin, so it's the best of both worlds.

- TENDERLOIN

The beef tenderloin is probably the most famous cut, which is sometimes called **filet mignon**. It can be pricey, so reserve this for special occasions. However, sometimes you can find it for about $5-6 a pound, which is a good deal.

- RIB EYE

If you are comfortable making it, just season the whole thing with a lot salt and pepper, sear the outside in a pan to brown, and place it in the oven at 400 degrees until the interior temperature is to your preference. A **standing rib roast** is a rack of prime ribs connected together, and the **rib eye** is the prime rib without the bone.

CONSIDER

- LONDON BROIL

If you are making fajitas or beef quesadillas, then this would be a good option to use, otherwise don't use it because it can be tough.

AVOID

- BRISKET

It takes a long time to cook, and you have some stiff competition with some grandmas. Just leave it for someone else.

- OXTAILS

This cut of meat is the toddler of the cow: very fatty, requires a lot of attention, takes a very long to become good and really expensive for something so small and stupid.

- BEEF RIBS

Again, these are very difficult to make. If you are looking to make ribs, purchase baby back ribs instead (see pg. 87).

STORE

I like to cut individual servings, place them in plastic bags and toss them into the freezer. This is a great trick for burgers! Buy the ground beef, season them and freeze them into individual burger patties. You can just place them frozen solid into your skillet.

TEMPERATURE

- RARE 135-140 degrees
- MEDIUM 140-150 degrees
- WELL DONE-170 and over

Pan con Bistec

MATERIALS
1 nonstick pan
1 pair of cooking tongs
Cutting board
Chef's knife
Plastic bag

INGREDIENTS
2 large boneless sirloin steaks, aka palomilla, pounded flat (you want enough to cover the bread)
1 loaf of Cuban, Puerto Rican or French baguette
1 vine ripe tomato
1 can crunchy potato strings
1 head of romaine lettuce
1 onion, thinly sliced
2 tablespoon olive oil
2 tablespoon balsamic vinegar
Adobo seasoning
Salt and pepper
Cooking spray

On certain days in high school, we would have pan con bistec for lunch, and it was on these days that I would run especially fast, pushing and shoving my way through the freshmen in order to be the first in line; if you arrived early enough, it was a simple matter of running to the front of line and piling on as many servings in your hands and pockets as you could carry.

Pan con bistec is a popular Cuban sandwich available at every Cuban restaurant in Miami. Traditionally, it is a thin steak served on Cuban bread with caramelized onions, lettuce, tomato, and crunchy potato strings. If you're a gringo like me, it's pronounced *ponn-con-bee-stake*.

20 minutes

COOKING THE ONIONS: Heat the pan with olive oil on medium high heat. Toss in the onions and season with salt and pepper. Sauté the onions for 10 minutes until they are the color of caramel and very soft, stirring every so often. When completed, remove them from the pan and set aside.

SMASHING THE STEAK: Place a plastic bag over a clean pan, and hit down onto the steak until the whole steak has thinned out. You don't want to kill it, just thin it out (to about ¼ inch in thickness) and a couple hits will be enough. This process will guarantee an evenly cooked steak, but remember you are not trying to attack a wild animal. Discard the plastic bag after you are done.

COOKING THE STEAK: On high heat, add the additional tablespoon of olive oil. Place the steak in the pan and coat it with balsamic vinegar. Allow the steak to sear for 2 to 3 minutes. Flip and repeat.

As the steak is cooking, slice the bread in half lengthwise, making sure not to cut all the way through. If you like, toast the bread until slightly brown. Slice tomatoes and lettuce. Remove the steak and allow it to rest on cutting board for a few minutes before assembling the sandwich.

ASSEMBLE THE SANDWICH: Line the bottom of the bread with a little bit of lettuce and place the steak on top. This will prevent the bread from getting soggy. Place the caramelized on top of the steak, and then add the remainder of the lettuce and tomato. Season the tomatoes with salt and pepper. Top with crunchy potato strings and serve hot.

MAKES 2 GIANT SANDWICHES

TIPS: Serve with French fries (*papitas fritas*).

Steak au Poivre

MATERIALS
An oven safe nonstick pan
Spatula
Plate
Cutting board

INGREDIENTS
Four 8 oz New York Strip steaks (about 1 inch thick)
¼ cup ground pepper
4 teaspoons salt
2 tablespoons butter
1 tablespoon olive oil

SAUCE
3 tablespoons butter
1 cup red wine
½ cup of beef broth

Steak au poivre (steak o pwahv) or steak with black pepper, is an easy French bistro dish that can be made in the oven, on the stovetop or on the grill. It is normally accompanied with a simple salade verte (green salad) and pomme frites (French fries). Substitute rib eye or filet mignon (beef tenderloin) for special occasions.

10-15 minutes

SEASON: Preheat the oven to 400 degrees. Place the salt and pepper on the plate and mix together with your finger. Dip the steaks into the mixture until they are completely coated on all sides. Repeat until all the steaks are coated.

SEAR: Melt the butter and olive oil in the pan on high heat. When butter is starting to brown, add the steaks. Do not touch them once they are in. Allow them to cook for 2 minutes, enabling a crust to form from the seasoning. After 2 minutes, flip them and place the pan in the oven.

Roast the steaks for another 5-8 minutes, until desired doneness is achieved. Allow them to rest, covered with aluminum foil, for 10 minutes before serving.

MAKES 4 SERVINGS

NOTE: For medium steaks, the internal temperature should be between 140-145 degrees. What does this mean? The interior should be slightly pink. The feeling of the steak should be slightly short of firm, meaning the meat springs back a little when you touch it. *If you close your non dominant fist tightly, it should feel as hard as the crevice between your thumb and index finger.*

WANT A SAUCE? Remove the steaks from the pan and on medium, high heat, add an additional 2 tablespoons of butter, 1 cup red wine and ½ cup of beef broth. Cook until the sauce has reduced into a thick syrup, about 5-7 minutes. Turn off the heat, add 1 more tablespoon of butter and drizzle it over the steaks.

EVOLUTION: Steak sandwich, quesadilla.

CARROTS: In the 2 tablespoons of the same oil that you used for the steak, add 4-5 thinly sliced carrots, 2 tablespoons

of brown sugar, salt and pepper. Cook for 7-10 minutes on medium high heat until the carrots are browned and fork tender. Drain on paper towel and serve.

Mongolian Beef

MATERIALS
Non stick pan
cutting board
Knife
Tongs
1 plate with paper towels for draining

INGREDIENTS
1 pound of hangar steak or skirt steak, thinly sliced
2 cloves garlic, minced
½ cup soy sauce
½ cup water
1 cup vegetable oil, plus 1 tablespoon oil
½ cup flour
1/3 cup brown sugar or white sugar
2 teaspoons sesame seeds (optional)
3 green onions (scallions) chopped into 1 inch pieces
Pepper

Chinese food is one of the easiest things to make because all you need is really high heat and a lot of salt.

The first time I tested this recipe was when I was doing a summer abroad in Italy, at 3 am right before we were heading to the airport. I was dead set on using all the food that we had purchased and because we didn't have a microwave, I had to pan-fry the steak to defrost it in time. The trick to the beef's crusty exterior and the thick sauce is the cornstarch, which can also be substituted with flour. Serve this with whatever you want, and add some spicy Thai chili sauce if you want some heat. PS: This is better version than the restaurant we'll call C. F. Shangs.

20 minutes

PREP: Slice the meat into thin pieces (they should be about the size of a cracker, and as thick as a grapefruit peel). *This can be done by cutting into the steak on a 45 degree angle. Hangar steak can be tough, so make sure to slice it across the grain. Try to make all the pieces uniform so that they cook at the same time.* Season the meat with pepper and coat with flour or cornstarch and allow it to sit while you mince the garlic and chop the scallions.

FRY: Heat the oil on high. Make sure the heat is pretty hot but not smoking. Add the meat. The meat should start to sizzle immediately, so immediately lower the heat to medium high. Cook until the outsides are crispy and brown, about 3-4 minutes. There is no need to turn the meat if it's covered in oil. *Don't cook it for longer than this otherwise the meat will dry out.*

USE THE SAME PLATE: When everything is cooked, drain the meat on the paper towel lined plate- just throw the flour into the garbage. The meat may not be completely cooked, but it will continue to cook afterwards so don't worry about it.

DRAIN: Remove all the oil from the pan. Discard it into a can, a jar, or dispenser that won't break if it has hot oil in it. Be careful as you are doing this. *DON'T pour the oil down the drain.*

SAUCE: In the same pan, on medium high heat, add garlic and scallions to the pan and cook for about 30 seconds. Add the soy sauce, water and sugar and stir. Cook the sauce for 5-7 minutes until it is thick and has formed a syrup- like consistency (*the heat should be relatively high to accomplish this, so don't lower it*). Add the meat back, and turn off the heat. Allow the meat to cook in the sauce for an additional 1-2 minutes. Add the sesame seeds and serve with white rice.

MAKES 2 SERVINGS

TIP: Cook white rice before you start slicing the meat, so that it will be finished at the same time. Use the microwave and it will take twenty minutes flat for three cups (pg. 116).

ADD SOME HEAT: Mongolian beef is typically made spicy, so if you like, add one whole spicy Thai chili or a couple hits of Tabasco sauce will do the trick.

Sausage and Beer

MATERIALS
A nonstick pan
Kitchen tongs
Toaster (or baking sheet for the oven)
Cutting board
Chef's knife
Can opener

INGREDIENTS
1 package of store bought sausages, about 6 (buy whatever you like, be it chicken sausage or spicy sausages, but I like sweet Italian sausages)
2 cans of beer
1 large onion, sliced
2 bell peppers, sliced
1 tablespoon of oil
One 12 oz can boiled potatoes
Salt and pepper
1 tablespoon paprika
1 package of hot dog buns

Beer is really a great ingredient and it's not just for drinking. I know shocking! Try adding it to beef stew, or using it instead of water to make a beer batter tempura. This recipe is not only great when you have extra beer but it's great for when you've had too much beer and you want to get something into your stomach. Eat the sausage by itself or in a hot dog bun with sautéed onions and peppers. The best thing about this recipe is that you have an entire meal in one pan.

15 minutes

PREP: Open the can of potatoes and drain the liquid. Slice the onions and peppers.

SAUTE: Bring the heat up to high. Add the onions, potatoes and peppers and sauté for 5 minutes, stirring constantly. Season with salt and pepper.

When the onions and peppers have started to brown and soften, add the sausages and the two cans of beer and cover. Continue to cook for about 10 minutes or until the liquid has almost completely evaporated. Season everything with salt and pepper. Every couple of minutes, turn the sausages so that they can brown on all sides.

When the sausages are browned on all sides, and the potatoes have developed a slight crust, remove them from the pan. The onions should be a nice golden color and the peppers should be soft as well.

TOAST (optional): As the sausages are cooking, toast the hot dog buns in the toaster or oven until golden brown. If you are in a hurry, broil the buns in the oven for about a minute. They cook quickly so watch out for them!

ASSEMBLE: Place the sausages on the buns, and top with onions and peppers, and eat with the potatoes. Serve with beer if you want.

MAKES 2-3 SERVINGS

TRY: This makes a great tailgating item. Cook the sausages in the pan with the beer until the liquid has completely evaporated, then finish browning them on the grill.

Meatballs

MATERIALS
A non stick pan
Large bowl
Spatula

INGREDIENTS
2 pounds ground beef*
1 cup parmesan cheese
½ panko bread crumbs, and additional ¼ cup if necessary
Cooking spray
¼ cup olive oil
3 tablespoon chopped basil, fresh is possible
3 tablespoons oregano
1 tablespoon parsley
2 tablespoons salt
2 tablespoon pepper
4 tablespoons of water (or 2 tablespoons of water and 2 tablespoons of balsamic vinegar)
1 egg

Every person and their mother (and grandmother for that matter) has a recipe for meatballs and I definitely don't want to compete against centuries' worth of history and secrecy. Instead, I would like to show you how to make basic, Italian style meatballs. The way I usually cook meatballs is in a tomato sauce, but because these often take a longer time to make, the second best way is to use the oven and just to throw them into the sauce when you're done.

A lot of traditional meatballs combine ground beef, pork and veal for the optimum level of fat and flavor, but I don't have $300 to spend on meatballs, so I omitted that idea.

25 minutes.

PREP: Preheat the oven to 400 degrees.

In the large bowl, combine all the ingredients together, along with half of the olive oil. Mix just so everything is combined, at most 1 minute. *It's important to not overwork the meat otherwise it will stiffen. The meatballs will be somewhat wet but don't worry about it because this will keep them moist when they cook.* Allow the meat to sit for about ten minutes so that the flavors can combine. Walk away.

FORM: Shape the meatballs with the palms of your hands, keeping them less than two inches in diameter. It is important that all the meatballs are about the same size, so that they cook for the same amount of time. Spray the nonstick pan with cooking spray and apply some oil- this will prevent the meatballs from sticking, and will also give color to the meatballs. Set the meatballs on the tray, leaving about two inches in between the meatballs as they cook.

BAKE: Bake the meatballs for 7-9 minutes. They should be cooked all the way through. If the meatballs are smaller, then they will cook faster, and vice-versa. Simply open one up at the 8 minutes to see if they are cooked through. If you are serving them in a tomato sauce, simmer the tomato sauce on low and add the meatballs until you are ready to serve.

If you already have a tomato sauce made and are planning on serving pasta with it, simply toss in the cooked pasta into the sauce to coat the pasta. The sauce will prevent the pasta from sticking together as you are waiting on the meatballs. Serve the meatballs on top.

MAKES ABOUT
32 MEATBALLS

Top right: Sausage and Beer.
Bottom left: Mini burgers.

Best Burgers

MATERIALS
1 large bowl
Tongs
1 baking sheet lined
with aluminum foil

INGREDIENTS
1 pounds beef
2 tablespoons salt
2 tablespoons pepper
2 tablespoons of
garlic powder
2 tablespoons basil

2 tablespoons
Worcestershire
sauce (optional)
2 tablespoons soy
sauce
2 tablespoons
balsamic vinegar
1 cup sweet Thai
chili sauce

These are called best burgers for a reason! Whenever you are grilling or searing burgers, remember not to press down on them, as this will cause the juices to run, leaving you with a dry hockey puck. And if you make too much, simply wrap the extras in individual bags and store in the freezer until you are ready to cook them off.

20 minutes (10 minutes for marinating)

COMBINE: In a large bowl, use your hands to combine all the ingredients together for exactly 1 minute. You don't want to overwork the meat otherwise the burgers will be stiff. *Do something else for 10 minutes so the flavors can combine.*

MOLD: **Preheat the broiler now.** Using the palms of your hand, form burger patties. Make sure the burgers are about the same size to ensure even cooking time.

BROIL/PAN FRY: After the broiler has been on for about 5 minutes, add the burgers. Cook the burgers on high broil, or pan fry on medium high in 2 tablespoons of oil, for about 3-5 minutes on each side, depending on the thickness. The burger should be firm and when pressed, should yield some resistance. *A 5 inch long burger about one inch thick should take about 4 minutes per side to cook to medium well.* Top the burgers with a dollop of sweet chili sauce each and allow them to cook for an additional minute until the sauce is hot.
Makes 4-5 Burgers/ 8-10 Sliders

Tacos

MATERIALS
A nonstick pan
Wooden spoon
Can opener
1 large spoon

INGREDIENTS
1 1/2 pounds of ground beef
1 large onion, sliced
2 tablespoon salt
2 tablespoon pepper
¼ cup of balsamic vinegar
1 cup salsa
2 tablespoon of paprika
2 tablespoon of garlic powder
A couple hits of Tabasco sauce (optional but recommended)
1 sweet potato (optional), peeled and diced
4 microwave fried maduro pieces, chopped (optional)

I've been one to have my occasional midnight taco runs, so I know the value of a good taco. This is a great recipe for quick leftovers, so make a lot for the next day.

20 minutes

ON THE STOVE: On high heat, add the oil along with the ground beef, onions and sweet potato (optional). The objective is to brown the beef, so with the wooden spoon, break up the pieces of meat and just let it sit in the pan. Season it liberally with salt and pepper and continue to cook.

After about 8-10 minutes, the meat should be browned. Drain the excess oil from the pan with the spoon and discard. Add the remaining spices and salsa. Continue to cook the meat for an additional 5-8 minutes. Add the maduros and cook for one minute until everything is evenly dispersed.

All the flavors should be combined and the liquid should all be evaporated. Taste and adjust the seasoning if necessary. Serve with toasted taco shells, tortilla wrappers or on top of nachos.

SERVES 4 PEOPLE

EVOLUTION: Mexican pasta, (pg. 163).

Shrimp Scampi

MATERIALS
A large pot (to boil water)
Non stick pan
Cutting board
Chef's knife
Strainer
Wooden spoon
Plate

INGREDIENTS
1 pound of medium sized (20/24) shrimp (or any size that is one sale at the grocery store)
1 pound linguini, spaghetti or fettuccini
1 lemon, juiced
3 large cloves garlic, minced
3 tablespoons olive oil
2 tablespoons butter (or additional 2 tablespoons of olive oil if unavailable)
1 medium vine ripe tomato, diced
1 tablespoon basil (fresh or dried)
1 cup dry white wine (optional but recommended)
Grated parmesan cheese
Salt and pepper
Water

This version of shrimp scampi combines classic Mediterranean flavors from both Spain and France. The sauce takes very little time to make, and shrimp makes it a quick and light dish. Buy shrimp from the grocery store that is already peeled and de-veined. Fresh shrimp will be soft and grey in color and smell salty like the sea. All seafood should be kept very cold (but not near water or else they will get soggy) until you are ready to use. Shrimp cooks very quickly, so pay attention!

20 minutes

PREP: Run cold water through the shrimp to remove some of the excess saltiness. Drain thoroughly and set them aside until ready to use.

FOR THE PASTA: Fill up the large pot with water, stopping about 3 inches from the rim of pot. Bring to a boil.

Use your sink- filling the pot with hot water from the sink will cut your boiling time in half. When water begins to boil, throw in a couple tablespoons of salt into water, and then throw in pasta. Remember not to 'season the water' until it is boiling, otherwise the salt will accumulate and ruin the bottom of your pot.

COOKING THE SHRIMP: Place the lemons in the microwave for 20 seconds so that they become easier to juice. Finely mince the garlic, dice the tomatoes and chop the basil into small pieces. Heat 2 tablespoons of olive oil and two tablespoons of butter in the pan on medium high heat. Add the garlic and cook for 2 minutes, stirring occasionally until the garlic is slightly cooked. Add the tomatoes and white wine and season with salt and pepper. Bring the pan up to high heat because boiling helps cook off the alcohol in the wine. Once you see the sauce bubble, lower the heat to medium.

Shrimp cooks very quickly, so when the pasta is halfway cooked, add the shrimp to the sauce. Bring the heat up to medium high and allow them to cook. They should take around 4 minutes to cook, but probably less.

Once the pasta is *al-dente*, drain the pasta into the strainer, then add it to the pan with shrimp. Add the basil and toss everything together and allow the sauce to thicken slightly from the heat of the pan. Serve immediately with parmesan cheese and one tablespoon of olive oil lightly drizzled on top. This goes great with simple crusty bread.

MAKES 6 LARGE SERVINGS

TIP: Drink the wine that you used for cooking.

EVOLUTION: This dish is fantastic baked in the oven. Remove some of the excess sauce from the dish and replace it with a light béchamel sauce (see pg. 148). Combine everything together in an oven safe dish and top with mozzarella cheese (or whatever you have). Bake at 350 degrees until cheese is browned and bubbly. Allow to sit for a few minutes before serving

BUYING SHRIMP

Shrimp are measured in numbers. For example, if you see something that says 20/24, that means there's approximately 20 to 24 shrimp per pound. Also remember that if you buy fresh shrimp from the grocery store, see if you can get them peeled and deveined, otherwise you'll have to pull out the digestive tract by yourself and that's pretty messy work.

Shrimp is available both pre cooked or raw, and the raw shrimp will be grey in color. These are pretty much a safe bet, and are definitely some of the most affordable, if not most widely available seafood option.

STORE: Shrimp can be stored cooked in the fridge or frozen. It's pretty resilient. Most of the time when you buy them on sale in the grocery store, they were frozen and thawed.

Eggplant Parmesan

MATERIALS
Oven safe pan
Spatula/kitchen tongs
1 cereal bowl
2 plates
Chef's knife
Cutting board
Paper towels
Fork

INGREDIENTS
One large eggplant, sliced
2 cups of panko breadcrumbs (or regular breadcrumbs)
Tempura batter (1 cup flour, 1 and 1/2 cup ice cold water, plus additional 2 tablespoons)

½ cup of parmesan cheese
1 tablespoon basil
1 tablespoon oregano
1 tablespoon pepper
½ cup vegetable oil
1 tablespoon olive oil
Salt and pepper.

Toppings
1 cup mozzarella cheese
1 cup tomato sauce

In a Bon Appétit interview, Sophia Loren, the famous Italian actress, said she craves crispy eggplant parmesan sandwiches when she's feeling naughty. I don't know how naughty one can get at 73, and I honestly don't want to know either, so I can't tell you whether or not this dish will help anyone's chances of getting lucky. This classic eggplant parmesan is improved with flakey panko breadcrumbs and grated parmesan cheese. For the full sandwich, serve between two slices of toasted ciabatta with a thin layer of pesto sauce.

20 minutes

PREP: Preheat oven to 350 degrees. Slice the eggplant widthwise into ¾ inch pieces and season with salt and pepper.

ASSEMBLE: The breading station. In a cereal bowl, combine flour and ice water to form a tempura batter- it should be as thick and as smooth as a cake batter, but please don't eat it raw. On another plate, combine breadcrumbs, parmesan cheese, oregano, basil, salt and pepper- this is the breading station. Finally on the last plate, place the paper towels- this is to drain the excess oil from the fried eggplant.

Add oil to pan and increase the heat to medium high. Move your hand six inches from the pan. If you can feel the heat from the pan, its ready (this should take about 2 minutes to heat up).

Coat the eggplant as follows: Place the eggplant in tempura batter and coat completely. Then move to breadcrumb mixture and coat completely as well. Take it directly from the breading station to the hot oil.

Drop the eggplant into the pan. It should begin to sizzle immediately, but should not splatter. If the oil starts to jump at you, lower the heat to medium and remove the pan from the heat. Allow it to cool for about a minute before adding the remaining eggplant (*remember that when you fry, the temperature of the oil will drop substantially once you add more items to the pan, so you don't want to bring the oil to too low of a heat otherwise the eggplant will absorb the oil instead of fry in it.*)

Cook for 5 minutes, flip and repeat. The eggplant should be golden brown. It may be necessary to lower the heat to medium as you flip so it doesn't burn before it is cooked.

Press the fork into the eggplant and if it is soft, it is done

cooking. Remove and allow it to drain. Discard the excess oil from the pan.

When the eggplant is completely drained, bring it back to pan and cover it with mozzarella cheese. Place it in the oven to melt the cheese, about 5-8 minutes. The top should be golden brown.

To preserve the crunchiness of eggplant, add the tomato sauce right before serving. Simply heat it up in the microwave or stove and pour over the eggplant. Serve hot.

MAKES 2 SERVINGS

IMPRESS: Convert into appetizers. Make eggplant "fries" and use the tomato sauce as a dipping sauce.

Pineapple Express Fried Rice

MATERIALS
Large non stick pan
Cutting board
Chef's knife
2 microwavable bowls
Wooden spoon

INGREDIENTS
3 cups of cooked white rice (the best one to use is called parboiled because it will fry better and maintain its texture, but use whatever you have)
½ cup oil
1 cup frozen corn
1 cup frozen peas
1 head of broccoli, trimmed
4 large carrots
1 large ripe tomato
1 regular onion, diced
2 limes, quartered
One 16 oz can of pineapple, reserving half the juice from the can
¾ cup of sweet Thai chili sauce (or sweet and sour sauce)
4 Tablespoons of yellow curry powder (available in almost all grocery stores in spice section, simply labeled as curry powder)
3 eggs
5 dashes Tabasco sauce (or one tablespoon of Thai freshred chili pepper- found in a jar)
Salt and pepper
1 pound of fresh shrimp or leftover chicken (optional)

This Americanized fried rice is inspired by all the flavors of Asia and is an excellent dish to serve large groups because it can be easily multiplied and is also vegetarian friendly (and vegan if you decide to omit the eggs). For a small dinner, garnish each plate with a freshly fried egg.

35 minutes

RICE: Cook the rice in a rice cooker (as directed) or in the microwave (see pg. 116 for full instructions).

VEGETABLES: While the rice is cooking, prepare the vegetables. Trim the head of broccoli into florets by removing the stalk and isolating the segments. Place it in a large bowl of water with the frozen corn and frozen peas and microwave everything for 3 minutes. Set it aside and the residual heat will ensure that broccoli is tender before cooking. Finish prepping by dicing the carrots, onion and tomato.

ASSEMBLE: On high heat, combine the onions and carrots. Cook for about 3 minutes, stirring frequently, until both are soft and slightly browned. Add the tomatoes and cook for about 30 seconds, then add the rice. Season the rice with the sweet Thai chili sauce and curry powder, making sure to break up the rice with the wooden spoon so that it doesn't form one large glob. Combine until all the rice turns a vibrant yellow-orange color. The rice should be slightly moist and shouldn't be clumping together.

Drain the water completely from the broccoli, corn and peas, and add to pan. Add pineapple and pineapple juice, as well as leftover chicken or fresh shrimp if desired. Cook until everything is combined. The shrimp should be pink in color, and should take no longer than 4 minutes to cook.

FOR THE SCRAMBLED EGGS: Push a portion of the rice to the side of the pan, leaving a part of the bottom of the pan exposed. Crack the eggs into the pan. They should immediately begin to sizzle. Using the wooden spoon, break the eggs and combine into the rest of the rice. Taste them and season with salt and pepper as desired. For some heat, add Tabasco sauce. Serve hot with lime quarters.

MAKES 8 SERVINGS

TIPS: Serve it for breakfast the next day with a fried egg on top.

RICE IS RICE, right?

All rice wasn't created equal.

Being half Asian and having grown up in Miami, I know rice. I grew up on long grain rice varieties, which are frequently used for side-dishes because they are general purpose and absorb moisture without becoming clumpy. Some examples are **Jasmine** rice and **Basmati** rice, which you usually find in Thai (Jasmine) and Indian (Basmati) restaurants.

Shorter rice varieties also tend to be starchier in texture and clump together very easily. Some examples include risotto rice, like the Italian **Arborio**, and paella rice, like the Spanish **Valencia**, should be used differently than their long grain counterparts. Short grained **sushi** rice also makes a great substitution when making risotto.

As for fried rice, I recommend **parboiled rice**, which is rice that has been boiled in its husk. Even when cooked, parboiled rice maintains its size and texture incredibly well, and remains firm even when incorporated with other liquids like soy sauce.

Finally, **wild rice** is discolored rice that is characteristic of the genus Zizania, **dirty rice** is a Cajun method of cooking rice that is often spicy and made with ground beef, and **brown rice** is a sensitive subject for me that we just won't talk about.

COOKING RICE

Rice is very easy to make in the microwave. First cover the rice with water and use your fingers to wash the kernels. A milky, white substance will form at the top. Continue to wash the kernels in the water and drain the water after 30 seconds. Repeat the process again, until the milky layer is obsolete.

In a microwavable bowl, combine the rice and water. The ratio for rice is 1 cup of rice to 1 1/3 cup of water. You can add salt or the juice of one lime if you also wish. Cook in the microwave for 20 minutes exactly. Allow it to sit for five minutes before serving it.

SIDES

Whipped Potatoes

MATERIALS
Stock pot
Cutting board
Chef's Knife
Peeler
Fork
Strainer (optional)
Wooden spoon or handheld mixer (if available)

INGREDIENTS
4 large potatoes (look for varieties like Russet or Yukon Gold)
Salt and pepper
2 stick of butter (*I know, but this is what makes it good.* You can use only 1 stick if you want)
¾ cup of milk (you may not need it all)
1/3 cup sour cream (optional)
Salt and pepper

Patrick: "Look through it. I think I covered everything."
She flips through the book quickly.
Lauren: "Um…"
Patrick (slightly offended): "What? Everything is there!"
Lauren: "No. You didn't tell me how to peel potatoes. I hate peeling potatoes!"

Sometimes making homemade mashed potatoes seems like a worthless cause because you can buy pre-packaged mashed potatoes in the grocery store. However, these ARE THE ABSOLUTE BEST POTATOES I'VE TASTED, ANYWHERE! Do not skimp on the butter, and remember taste these as you cook. You will have to adjust the seasoning.

25 minutes

BOIL: Peel the potatoes and dice them into small pieces- the smaller you dice the potatoes, the faster they'll cook. Place the potatoes in the pot and cover them with water. There should be about two extra inches of water over the potatoes. Bring the pot up to a boil.

When the water is boiling, add a teaspoon of salt into the water to season the potatoes. Cook for about 15-20 minutes. To check for doneness, use a fork and press into the potatoes. If the potatoes have no resistance, and are beginnings to fall apart, they are done. (Most chefs would discourage cooking the potatoes for so long, but they're getting mashed anyways so it doesn't matter).

Drain the excess water from the potatoes, leaving as little as possible. This can be done by simply placing your knife at the edge of the pot so that water can seep through, while the knife catches the potatoes or by using a strainer.

COMPLETE: Add the potatoes to the pot and bring the heat up to medium. The heat will begin to evaporate any excess water. Melt the butter into the potatoes. On low speed, begin by whipping the potatoes by hand (or hand mixer), gradually adding milk about a quarter cup at a time. The potatoes should start to take shape and combine. Keep adding liquid until the mixture is completely combined, but not so that the potatoes become runny- you may not need all the milk. (*Don't worry if you don't have a handheld mixer because the potatoes will still be very easy to mash. Use a wooden spoon instead*). Whip in the sour cream and season with salt and pepper. Serve, or combine with condiments.

PEELING POTATOES: *If you hate peeling potatoes, you will need two large bowls filled with water. Place one in the microwave and heat it up until the water is boiling. Add several handfuls of ice to the second bowl. When the water is boiling, add the washed potatoes to the bowl and let them sit for about 30 seconds. Using kitchen tongs, remove them from the boiling water and add them to the ice water. Let them sit in the ice water for another 30 seconds. The skin should slide right off.*

MAKES 3-4 SERVINGS

NOTE: Most people think that when you boil potatoes, you should wait until the water is boiling, but if you do that, the outsides of the potatoes will be falling apart and the inside will still be firm and undercooked. Allowing them to start cooking when the water is still cold will prevent this from happening

Garlic and Parmesan Whipped Potatoes

INGREDIENTS   3 cloves garlic, minced   ½ cup of parmesan cheese

COOK: Follow the direction for basic whipped potatoes. However, mince garlic into small pieces and add it to the potatoes right before you are ready to boil them. Continue through the steps: the garlic will soften in the boiled water, and will infuse the potatoes with their flavor. Whip potatoes and right before you are ready to serve. Add parmesan cheese and stir until just combined.

Wasabi Whipped Potatoes

MATERIALS
1 cereal bowl
1 spoon

INGREDIENTS
2 tablespoon of wasabi powder

1 teaspoon (or less) of water

COOK: Follow the directions for basic whipped potatoes. Towards the end, combine a very small amount of water with wasabi powder just so that it forms a paste. Combine the paste into the potatoes and stir until thoroughly combined. Serve, or keep warm until ready to serve.

NOTE: Wasabi is available in tubes at the grocery store, so simply squeeze two teaspoons, taste and add more if you like.

Couscous

If I were to describe couscous for the first time, it's almost the combination of rice and pasta. It's made with semolina (which is a type of wheat that is also used for pastas) but it cooks like rice in the fact that is absorbs water. Couscous is most commonly associated with Moroccan cuisine, but is widely used in North Africa and the Middle East. The benefit of couscous is that it cooks quickly, and yet it still holds its shape. Serve it as a hot side dish, or as a cold salad, and it can serve as a great vegetarian option as well.

5 minutes to cook

Couscous is deceiving in size, so don't go overboard. Buy a pre seasoned package and safe yourself the trouble.

The optimal ratio of water to couscous, again, depends on what type of couscous you are using (Israeli couscous is much thicker). *You can also substitute chicken stock for water.* If you are buying the pre cooked couscous, it usually comes with directions, but if you are buying a regular container, I find that the ratio is usually 1/4 cup of couscous to 1 cup of water.

1 cup of couscous makes about 3-4 servings.

DIRECTION TO COOK:

MICROWAVE: Fill a microwavable bowl with the corresponding amount of water. Don't add the couscous yet! If you are making 1 cup of couscous, fill the bowl with about 1 ¼ cups of water because the microwave will evaporate some of it. Cook on high for 5 minutes until the water is boiling.

Remove it from the microwave, add the couscous and cover the bowl Add a pinch of salt, pepper, 2 tablespoons of butter or olive oil, garlic powder, and some freshly chopped parsley if you like. Allow it to sit for five minutes. When it is done, use your fork and fluff it up.

ADD WHAT YOU LIKE: Couscous serves as a great medium for a lot of dishes. Here are some great options for you to try (each recipe is intended for 1 cup of uncooked couscous, or about 2 ½ cups cooked couscous):

BACON, TOMATOES, RED ONION AND CUCUMBER: season the couscous with some oregano and mix in 1 cup of quartered cherry tomatoes, ½ red onion thinly sliced, ¼ cup of fresh basil or parsley chopped, and a carrot (optional). Finish with ¼ cup lemon juice and 1/3 cup of olive oil. Season well with salt and pepper.

couscous (besides the craisins, which I prefer to raisins). Use chicken broth instead of water for this recipe, and season the couscous with a tablespoon of curry powder (the yellow stuff). Combine 1/2 cup craisins along with ½ cup of toasted pine nuts (or cashews). Finish with ¼ cup of lemon juice and ¼ cup olive oil. Season with salt and pepper, and serve whenever you want.

ROASTED SWEET POTATO, BACON AND PECANS; Skin and chop the sweet potatoes into bite size pieces and sauté in a pan with a couple tablespoons of butter. Cook until fork tender. Add 4 strips of crispy, chopped bacon and ½ cup of toasted walnuts to cooked couscous.

CURRIED COUSCOUS WITH CRAISINS, BACON AND DATES- This recipe is perhaps the most traditional preparation for

Bacon Wrapped Corn

MATERIALS
1 baking sheet

INGREDIENTS
4 cobs of corn, removed from the husk
4 slices of bacon
2 tablespoons of butter
Salt and pepper
2 tablespoons of olive oil or cooking spray

This is probably one of the easiest recipes in this book, as well as one of the most satisfying. It is a great item to make during the summer when corn is at its ripest, and also fantastic for tailgating. If you don't have fresh corn, you could always use frozen corn and crumble in bits of bacon but this is one of the few times that fresh corn triumphs over frozen.

18 minutes

Preheat the oven to 400 degrees.

As the oven is preheating, take the butter in your fingers and rub it all over the corn. Rub it down! When you are done, wash your hands then season the corn all over with salt and pepper.

WRAP IT UP: Spray the baking sheet with cooking spray or with olive oil to prevent the bacon from sticking to it.

Wrap one strip of bacon around each cob of corn, making sure that the corn sits over the ends of the bacon as it cooks so that it doesn't move.

BAKE or ROAST: Cook the corn for 8 minutes, then flip it over so the other side of bacon can crisp up. Allow it to cook for an additional 5 minutes or until the bacon is crispy.

Remove it from the oven and allow the corn to cool for a couple minutes. Serve.

MAKES 4 SERVINGS

Creamed Spinach

MATERIALS
A nonstick pan
Microwavable bowl
Cutting board
Chef's knife
1 strainer or 1 clean kitchen towel
Wooden spoon

INGREDIENTS
2 packages frozen spinach
4 Tablespoons of butter (half a stick)
3 cloves garlic
2 cup milk
2 oz cream cheese
2-3 shots of Maggi seasoning (optional but recommended)
½ cup of parmesan cheese
Salt and pepper

One of my favorite creamed spinach recipes comes from The Palm Steakhouses, but I'm not an idiot, so I'm not going to pay $11 a serving when I can make 4 servings at home for $5. I tried to improve on the recipe as well as create a healthier option and the resulting creamed spinach is a smooth, rich side dish that even people who hate spinach would love. It is also better than the Palm. Seriously! This spinach also forms the base for the spinach and artichoke dip.

30 minutes (defrosting spinach takes 12)

PREP: In a microwavable bowl, place the two packages of spinach with ¼ cup of water. Cook as directed by the package instructions, about 7 minutes per package or about 12 minutes for both packages. Every couple of minutes, stir the spinach with a spoon.

When the spinach is defrosted, ring out the excess liquid. This can be accomplished by putting the spinach in the kitchen towel and ringing it over the sink until all the liquid is released, or by putting spinach in a colander and pushing the liquid out with your fist. Once finished, place the spinach on the cutting board and chop it into small pieces. It doesn't have to be perfect but try and chop it as thoroughly as possible, as this will help create the desired texture.

COOK: On medium high heat, melt the butter in the pan. Add the garlic and cook just until it begins to brown. Add the spinach and one cup of milk and bring the mixture to a simmer (you may need to increase the heat slightly). Continue to stir until the milk has completely dissolved, about 10 minutes. Season with salt and pepper. Add the remaining cup of milk and continue to cook until completely dissolved. I know it's a pain to add the milk in parts, but it doesn't come out the same if you add it all at the same time.

When the milk is almost completely dissolved, cut the cream cheese into small pieces and scatter it throughout spinach. The heat from the spinach should begin to melt the cream cheese, and the mixture should adopt a slightly thicker consistency. Taste and season as desired. Serve immediately.

MAKES 4 SERVINGS

IMPRESS: Drizzle with truffle oil. (I know, where the f**k am I going to find truffle oil but you can get it at Marshall's).

EVOLUTION: Leftovers make excellent fillers to omelets. See spinach and artichoke dip (next page).

Spinach and Artichoke Dip

MATERIALS
Microwavable plate
Paper towels
Oven safe dish

INGREDIENTS
One 15 oz can artichokes, chopped
4 strips bacon
5 slices of a good melting cheese (such as Mozzarella, Swiss, Gruyere, Provolone or Muenster)

Follow the same recipe from above to create this dip, which is best served hot with baked pita chips.

ASSEMBLE: Preheat the oven to broil.

Follow the directions from above, but also place 4 strips of bacon on a microwavable plate for 4 minutes or until brown and crunchy. Set aside to cool.

Chop the artichokes into small, bite size pieces and add it to the garlic and butter right before you add the spinach. Sauté for 2 minutes, until the artichokes are just slightly browned. After adding the cream cheese, add the crumbled bacon to the mixture. Combine until there are pieces of bacon throughout.

Top the mixture with cheese so that it covers every bite. Place the oven safe dish in the oven and broil until the top of the cheese is melted and brown. Serve the dip hot.

NOTE: Serve with a spoon just in case the cheese is too thick to just swoop down and eat the dip.

EVOLUTION: Toast an English muffin and top with spinach mixture. Place a slice of ham on top, along with some scrambled eggs, and you have a deconstructed Eggs Benedict.

MAKES 4-6 APPETIZER SERVINGS

Mashed Sweet Potatoes with Bacon

MATERIALS
2 microwavable plates
1 spoon
Cutting board
Knife

1 fork
Paper towels

INGREDIENTS
4 large sweet potato
3 strips of bacon

3 tablespoons butter
Salt and pepper
1 cup toasted pecans, chopped

At the suggestion of one of my friends, I tried to make several recipes for the microwave. This dish, from start to end, is completely made in the microwave, but don't let that distract you.

The technique I incorporated for this dish was inspired by Thomas Keller's butternut squash agnolotti, and this potato mixture can be turned into a great appetizer with some wonton wrappers.

35 minutes

COOK: Line a microwavable plate with paper towels and place on the strips of bacon. Cook for 3 minutes or until the bacon is brown and crunchy. Remove it from then microwave and set aside.

Spear the potatoes repeatedly with a fork. Don't worry, they don't have feelings. Cook for 17-20 minutes. They will make a sound like a soft sizzling from the inside of the microwave, but nothing is going to blow up.

Let them cool for 5-10 minutes.

ASSEMBLE: Chop the pecans into small pieces and set aside. When the potatoes are done, remove and cut in half to release some of the heat. Carefully, remove the potatoes from the bowl and place them on the cutting board.

Skin the potatoes: Use the spoon, and along one side of the potato, pull along the skin until you're left with the flesh. Place the flesh inside the bowl and continue until finished. Crumble the bacon with your fingers, and combine it with potato, butter, pecans, salt and pepper. The heat from the potatoes should melt the butter. Stir until the mixture is smooth and serve.

MAKES 4 SERVINGS

IMPRESS: Place the potato mixture into a baking dish. Instead of adding pecans to the mixture, top it with pecans and add a generous sprinkle of brown sugar and several tablespoons of butter (about 2-3). Cook at 350 degrees for 20 minutes until the pecans are brown and the sugar has formed a thick syrup atop the potatoes.

REALLY IMPRESS: Use the mixture as a filler for wonton wrapper to make homemade ravioli. Serve with sage butter sauce, pg. 151.

NOTE: Sweet potatoes have a lot of sugar in them, so when you cook them in the microwave, they will release a lot of liquid. Once you take the potatoes out and place them on the cutting board, run water over the plate so the sugar doesn't have a chance to crystallize and harden. This will make your clean up easier.

Roasted Broccoli with Parmesan

MATERIALS
Cereal bowl
Kitchen tongs
Cutting board
Chef's knife

INGREDIENTS
1/4 cup of olive oil
1 head of broccoli
Salt and pepper
½ cup of Parmesan cheese

1 teaspoon dried basil (optional)
3 cloves of garlic (whole)
2 slices of salami (optional but recommended)

Out of all the vegetables ever cultivated by man, broccoli by far has the worst reputation. Eaten raw, it's disgusting, and eaten steamed, it doesn't taste like anything. But when roasted or fried, it adapts a completely new flavor. Unfortunately, frozen broccoli doesn't work for this recipe because the broccoli will turn too soft after it is defrosted. The secret to this is simplicity; try it as a side dish, and you won't have any leftovers. This recipe is actually sautéed because it's faster, but feel free to roast at 400 degrees for 20 minutes as well.

15 minutes

ASSEMBLE: Trim the broccoli. See pg. 229 for step by step instructions. It doesn't have to be perfect, so don't stress about it.

The only thing you're looking for is uniformity, which will ensure an equal cooking time for all the broccoli pieces.

BLANCH: Place the broccoli in the microwave and cook for 2 minutes. Allow it to cool for about 2 minutes then drain out the liquid.

SAUTE: Heat up the olive oil on high heat and throw in the garlic, pepper flakes and basil to infuse into the oil. You don't need to let it heat up for that long, only about one minute.

Add the broccoli, season with salt and pepper and cook. Don't toss the broccoli around took much because you want it to get slightly brown around the edges. Cook for only 5 minutes.

You still want it somewhat crunchy.

Remove the broccoli from the pan and sprinkle with parmesan cheese. Take out the garlic clove, if you like, but you won't eat it anyways. Drizzle a little bit of olive oil on top and serve hot.

MAKES 2-3 SERVINGS

Sautéed String Beans

MATERIALS
Nonstick pan
Kitchen tongs
Cutting board
Chef's knife
Microwavable bowl

INGREDIENTS
12-16 oz of string beans (one package)
2 cloves garlic, minced
¼ cup freshly grated parmesan cheese
1 tablespoons butter
1 tablespoon of olive oil
1 lemon, juiced and zested (zesting is optional)
Salt and pepper

String beans make a great, simple side dish to any main course, and using the microwave-blanching method, these string beans take no time at all to make. Because string beans have a very muted flavor, feel free to combine them with anything you want. This French inspired recipe can serve as a base to build upon with your favorite ingredients.

10 minutes

PREP: Trim the tips off of the string beans. See pg. 230 for instructions.

Place them in a microwavable bowl filled with water so that everything is covered, and add a pinch of salt. Microwave for 3 minutes, or until the string beans are tender. Drain the hot water from the bowl and then add ice and splash them with cold water. We're just trying to stop the cooking process so they maintain their color. When the string beans are cold, dry them off.

SAUTE: On medium heat, melt the butter and oil in a non stick pan. As the butter is melting, peel and finely mince garlic. Add garlic to pan and cook for 2-3 minutes, until it is translucent and has infused its flavor. If the garlic starts to brown, lower the heat and continue stirring.

Add the string beans and lemon juice. Cut thin slices into the skin of the lemon half and add it to the pan as well. *The flavor of the lemon is highly concentrated in the zest, or outer layer of the lemon, and scoring it (or cutting gently into it) will help release the natural oils.*

Bring the heat up to high and cook until most of the liquid has evaporated, about 5 minutes. Season with salt and pepper.

Serve with grated parmesan cheese and serve immediately.

MAKES 2-3 SERVINGS

IMPRESS: Toast ¼ cup slivered almonds, walnut or cashews and add to string beans (but don't buy them if you don't have them).
For a spicier sauce, add 2 tablespoons paprika and 1 teaspoon red pepper flakes butter as it melts.

EVOLUTION: Serve on a salad the next day. If you're feeling really fancy, preheat the oven to 200 degrees and place the string beans (omit liquid) on a baking sheet. Dehydrate the string beans for two hours, until the beans are crunchy. Check for seasoning and eat them as a snack. PS You can also buy this at Whole Foods, but you might have to sell your car first.

Black Beans

MATERIALS
A nonstick pan
Cutting board
Chef's knife
Wooden spoon

INGREDIENTS
One 12 oz can black beans
Half of a white onion, dice
2 tablespoons olive oil
2 cloves garlic, minced
1 tablespoons paprika (optional)
1 bay leaf (if available, but don't go out to buy it if you don't have it)
1 teaspoon basil
5 shots of Tabasco sauce
1 lime quartered
Salt and pepper

Black beans, or frijoles negros, are everywhere in Miami, and I'm sure if you looked hard enough, you'd find someone named Black Bean. They're a feature on every Spanish menu because they are both cheap and can be made in large quantities. Beans also stay well in the fridge for a long time and make a great vegetarian option because they're really high in protein and fiber.

12 minutes

SAUTE: Heat the olive oil on medium high heat. Dice the onion and add it to the pan with the minced garlic. Cook for 3 minutes until both items are soft and translucent but not browned. Add the entire can of black beans to the pan. Season with pepper, the bay leaf, basil and Tabasco sauce. Beans are salty, so don't salt until after you've tasted them at the very end.

Allow the beans to simmer on medium heat for 5 to 7 minutes. Taste and season (and salt if necessary). I like to add about a teaspoon of pepper to this dish. When you're ready to serve, remove the bay leaf and discard. Serve with a squeeze of lime juice.

MAKES 3 SERVINGS

IMPRESS: Melt a sharp cheddar cheese atop beans before serving.

Spanish Style Chickpeas

MATERIALS
1 pan
Cutting board
Knife
Wooden spoon

INGREDIENTS
One 15.5 oz can of chickpeas (also called garbanzos), drained
1 4 oz can of tomato sauce (the smallest can, NOT paste)
2 tablespoons olive oil
Half a medium onion, chopped
2 cloves garlic, minced
1 tablespoon paprika
1 teaspoon curry powder
1 teaspoon cumin (optional)
Pepper to taste

Chickpeas are a great vegetarian option because they are very high in protein. Tomatoes also contain lycopene, which has shown to help prevent cancer; heated tomatoes were even suggested to reduce the clogging of arteries. Served with white rice, this option is an incredibly easy main course that can easily become a great side dish.

18 minutes

START: Heat up the pan on medium heat. Chop the onions and the mince the garlic and add them to the pan. Cook for 3 minutes until the onions are soft and translucent and the garlic is brown but not burned.

Drain the excess liquid from the chickpeas, leaving only the chickpeas in the can. They should smell briny. Rinse them out thoroughly with water because there is a lot of salt in the liquid. When they are clean, the briny smell should be completely muted.

Bring the heat up to medium-high. Add the chickpeas to the pan and sauté for a minute. Then add the tomato sauce, paprika, curry powder and cumin. The chickpeas will probably not need any salt, but season with pepper.

Simmer on medium low heat for 10-12 minutes. The liquid should have reduced and the flavor should be concentrated.

Taste and season again. Serve. This recipe can be kept in the refrigerator for a week.

MAKES 2 SERVINGS

TRY: Carrots for added sweetness. Also, blend leftovers with ½ cup olive oil for a great tomato hummus.

IMPRESS: Add 1/3 cup of sliced chorizo.

Roasted Potatoes with Cheddar Dipping sauce

MATERIALS
1 baking sheet
Tongs
Cutting board
Knife

INGREDIENTS
4 large potatoes (Russet or Yukon Gold)
1 teaspoon salt
1 teaspoon pepper
1 tablespoon rosemary
1 teaspoon basil (optional)
½ cup olive oil
2 cloves of garlic, whole

Many restaurants serve potatoes covered with bacon and cheddar cheese, and in Men's Health magazine, a famous version of this recipe featured prominently in a chain that is known by a day of the week turned out to be more than 1000 calories an order. This healthier option will break the monotony a little bit with roasted potatoes and offer you some of what you're craving without the unnecessary extras.

30 minutes

FOR THE POTATOES: Preheat the oven to roast at 400 degrees. Wash the potatoes. Because we're leaving the skins on, try and take all the grit that might have accumulated. Cut the potatoes into two-bite pieces (lengthwise is good, but don't go crazy over you chopping). Make sure that the potatoes are all relatively the same size so that they cook at the same time. Coat the potatoes with oil and season with rosemary, basil and liberally with salt and pepper on all sides. Toss with your fingers on the baking sheet and add the garlic. Roast potatoes for 30 minutes, or until fork tender and slightly crispy. Serve hot with cheddar dipping sauce (next page).

MAKES 4 SERVINGS

Fondue Cheese Sauce

MATERIALS
1 pot (which acts as
the serving bowl)
1 wooden spoon
Cheese grater

INGREDIENTS
12 oz. of favorite
melting cheese,
grated
Salt and pepper

1 cup of milk
½ stick of butter
2 tablespoons of
flour

The best fondues are made mostly of cheese, melted slowly with just a touch of milk to thin them out. Select your favorite melting cheese, or purchase one of those variety bags.

10 minutes

FONDUE: Grate the cheese. This is a crucial step, otherwise the cheese will never melt. On medium heat, combine the butter and flour for 1 minute, just until a roux is formed (the butter and flour should combine together into a light brown paste). Add the milk and the grated cheese and continue to stir for 5-7 minutes, depending on the cheese variety and how fast it melts. Thin the cheese out with extra milk if necessary, but you may not need it all. It is important to remember to not try to melt it too quickly otherwise the cheese will scald to the bottom of the pan. Season with pepper and serve. Serve with sliced green apples, pieces of French bread, blanched broccoli etc.

MAKES 2-3 SERVINGS

Choose a good melting cheese with flavor: If you are looking to save on money, buy a variety bag. Look for cheeses like havarti, fontina, gruyere and comte. Don't buy mozzarella. PS I researched this point, and all of the best restaurants agree on comte as the best.

Sautéed Mushrooms

MATERIALS
A nonstick pan
Wooden spoon
Cutting board
Chef's knife

INGREDIENTS
1 package of store bought mushrooms, cleaned and sliced (if available and on sale, buy shiitake, baby Portobello or crimini, but white button mushrooms are fine)
1 cup of dry red wine (or ½ cup of beef stock)
1 tablespoon rosemary
3 tablespoons butter
Salt and pepper

The first time I ever ate mushroom, I had them in a mushroom soup and I haven't looked back since. For some reason, I've noticed a lot of people don't like mushrooms or olives, and trust me, olives are harder to eat than mushrooms. Sautéed with butter, rosemary and red wine, these mushrooms take on a completely different flavor than the regular salad condiment. Use this recipe as a side dish, a burger or pizza topping, or even a filler for vegetarian lasagna.

20 minutes

TO PREP: Slice mushrooms into 1/8 inch slices (you can also buy them pre-sliced). To do so, simply cut the mushroom in half so you have a flat surface, and run your knife across to make thin slices.

SAUTE: Melt two tablespoons of butter in a pan on medium high heat. Add mushroom and bring the heat all the way up. (Mushrooms have a lot of moisture in them, and the heat from the pan and salt will help release the moisture). However, because you want color on the mushrooms, allow them to cook for 5-7 minutes, or until golden brown in color, before you salt them. When some of their moisture starts to be released and they are golden brown, add the wine.

Make sure that the mixture is boiling slightly to evaporate some of the alcohol. Season the mixture with salt, pepper and rosemary (crumble rosemary between your fingers as you add it into the pan). Once boiling, bring the heat down slightly to medium high. The mixture doesn't need to be boiling, but we are trying to reduce the liquid in the pan. Cook for about 4 minutes.

REDUCE THE SAUCE: When the wine has reduced to a thick syrup (there should be about 1/8 cup of liquid still left in the pan), turn off the heat and add the last tablespoon of butter. Taste and adjust the seasoning if needed. Serve.

MAKES 2-3 SERVINGS

TRY: If you don't have access to red wine, use beef stock with 2 tablespoons of balsamic vinegar in them. Reduce them in the same manner as the wine.

NOTE: To clean the mushrooms, rub them with a damp paper towel to remove some of the dirt. Don't soak them in water otherwise they will absorb it like a sponge and lose all of their flavor.

Roasted Asparagus

MATERIALS
1 Nonstick pan
Tongs
1 Chef's knife

INGREDIENTS
1 package of asparagus
1 teaspoon salt
1 teaspoon pepper
Olive oil to coat

If you like asparagus, then roasted asparagus will become your new best friend. But if you hate asparagus, then roasted asparagus could become the only way you'll ever eat it. This roasted asparagus is ridiculously simple to make, and if you are fancy, with just a couple cups of chicken stock, a blender and some cream, this roasted asparagus turns into a fantastic soup.

15 minutes

ROAST: Preheat the oven to 400 degrees.

Snap off the ends of the asparagus- the bottoms of the asparagus are pretty tough, so you don't want to eat them. Here's the trick: Snap the end off one of the asparagus, and line all of them up together. Then use the length of the snapped asparagus as a ruler for the others. All you need is one slice and all the asparagus are finished (see pg. 232 for further directions).

Place the asparagus on the tray and season with salt and pepper. Drizzle a couple tablespoons of oil onto the tray and roll the asparagus around. The oil will help them brown and crisp.

Roast for 12-15 minutes, depending on the size. Toss them around half way through the roasting to ensure that they don't stick. When they are finished, the asparagus will become slightly browned and crispy. Serve hot.

MAKES 2-3 SERVINGS

PASTA

Clockwise (top left): Bolognese, Italian Sausage with broccoli and carrots, Tuscan pesto, Shrimp with Asparagus and Rigatoni with artichokes and peas.

Clockwise (top left): Pesto, Shrimp with Bruschetta, Frutti di Mare, Ravioli with Sage butter and Sausage with caramelized onions.

21 Pastas in 20 Minutes

MATERIALS
Non stick pan
Pot
Wooden spoon
Colander

Cutting board
Chef's knife

INGREDIENTS
½ pound of pasta *

Olive oil
Salt and pepper
Parmesan cheese

All of these pastas can be made in less than 20 minutes. Simply boil the water first and make the sauce while the pasta is cooking. To boil water even faster, use the sink: tap water will heat up faster than if you were to boil it on the stove.

When the pasta is al dente (meaning that the outside is tender and soft but the core of the pasta is very slightly chewy), simply drain and toss it in the sauce before serving.

Before you start making pasta, here are some things to keep in mind:

EACH RECIPE YIELDS 2 SERVINGS

KEEP IT SIMPLE. Sometimes four ingredients are all you need. Use seasonal items to get the best quality. Look through your pantry and freezer for ideas.

WATCH YOUR LEFTOVERS. Keep in mind that many proteins will be less moist the next day and all they need is to simply be heated through. Items like steak are best rarer, and are best served cold and simply sliced on top of pasta (as the heat of the pasta will warm it through). My favorite type of protein to use is leftover chicken, because it is flavorful and yet doesn't compete with the other ingredient.

YOU DON'T ALWAYS NEED SAUCE. Simply adding leftover pasta water to the hot pan will thicken some of the tidbits that might have formed on the bottom; scrape them to release, which is a technique called *deglazing*. Remember, sauces should coat pasta, not drown them. If anything, finish the pasta with olive oil and grated cheese, and you're done.

SEASON THE WATER. Throw in a couple tablespoons of salt in the pasta water. Italian chefs believe the pasta water should always taste like the sea. If this makes you feel guilty, remember that Italians have some of the longest life expectancy in the world.

WINE MAKES IT BETTER. I am not trying to start a new wave of underage drinking, but if you have any leftover red or white wine, most of these recipes will be that much better. Invest.

Basic Tomato Sauce

MATERIALS
Non stick pan
Cutting board
Chef's knife
Wooden spoon

INGREDIENTS
1 28 oz can of crushed tomatoes
1 medium size onion, diced
3 cloves garlic
Half a package of fresh basil (it really makes a difference to buy this)
2 carrots, peeled and diced
Salt and pepper
½ cup olive oil
2 tablespoons balsamic vinegar (or a splash of red wine)
2 tablespoons of sugar
1 teaspoon oregano (optional)

The basic tomato sauce, or *salsa di pomodoro*, needs no explanation. Use this sauce for both pasta and pizza, or simply warmed up and eaten with toasted bread for a snack. Make this sauce once at the beginning of the year, and save the remainder of it in small containers for the freezer. It will save you a lot of money over time. When you need it, simply take it out of the freezer and warm it up in the microwave.

25 minutes

FOR THE SAUCE: Heat up the olive oil on medium heat. Dice the onion and carrots, mince the garlic, and add them to the pan. Cook for about 5 minutes, making sure the garlic doesn't burn. Add the tomatoes and balsamic vinegar. Cover the pot to prevent splattering then bring everything to a boil. As soon as the sauce is boiling, drop the heat down to low. Remove the stems from the basil, (leaving on the leaves) and chop it into small pieces. Add the basil and season the sauce with salt and pepper. Allow everything to simmer on low for about 20 minutes. Taste and adjust seasoning if necessary. Serve immediately or place in the freezer to store.

YIELDS ABOUT 3 CUPS OF SAUCE.

TRY: The carrots will make this sauce slightly chunky, so feel free to blend the sauce in the food processor.

NOTE: In many grocery stores around the country, you can find canned tomatoes from Italy. The best are from **San Marzano**, but check the label for other tomatoes like these. They will be more expensive (maybe 50 cents to a dollar more), but these tomatoes have a higher sugar concentration than American ones and will result in a sweeter, better tasting sauce. The purpose of the balsamic vinegar is to supplement the sweetness when using regular tomatoes.

EVOLUTION:

TOMATO CREAM SAUCE- Add about 3 tablespoons of cream (or half and half) for every 1 cup of sauce.

VODKA SAUCE- Follow the basic tomato cream sauce recipe plus 2 tablespoons of vodka per cup in addition. Make sure you bring up the sauce up to a boil to evaporate some of the alcohol. If you haven't had this before, please note that it will not taste like the drink in your hand, so don't expect it to.

Béchamel Sauce

MATERIALS
1 nonstick pan
1 wooden spoon

INGREDIENTS
4 tablespoons butter
2 heaping tablespoons flour
1 1/2 cups milk (or cream)
1 teaspoon nutmeg (this is a classic spice for bechamel, but it's optional)
Salt and pepper

A béchamel sauce is really a cream sauce, or an Alfredo sauce without the cheese. It is one of the four main French "mother sauces" and can evolve into a bunch of other sauces. It can be used as a base for macaroni and cheese, white pizzas, nacho toppings and can be combined with pureed vegetables to make a bisque (like with lobster, asparagus etc.). My advice is to master this recipe and it will take you far.

12 minutes

IN THE PAN: Melt butter on medium-high heat. Once the butter is completely melted, about 1 minute, add the flour. You are now making a **roux**, which is the light brown paste that forms when melted butter and flour combine.

Cook the roux for about 45 seconds, stirring with a whisk or spoon, until the butter and flour are mixed. It should be yellow in color, and slightly thick. It should not be lumpy and the flour should be completely dissolved into it.

Add the milk (or cream), season with salt, pepper and nutmeg, and bring the sauce to a boil. Once bubbles start to form at the top, reduce the heat to medium, continually stirring every so often. The sauce will continue to thicken. Once the mixture has been cooking for about 5 minutes, it should be able to coat the back of the spoon. When it does, it is done. This is the time when you could add cheese to it. Serve hot.

YIELDS ABOUT 1 ½ CUPS OF SAUCE.

NOTE: The longer you cook the roux, the darker it will be and the less thick the resulting dish becomes.

EVOLUTION:

ALFREDO SAUCE: Add cheeses like a handful of mozzarella (for thickness) and 1/3 cup of parmesan (for flavor) and allow them melt for a minute on medium heat, right after the béchamel has thickened.

NACHO/MAC AND CHEESE SAUCE: Add one handful of sharp cheddar and one handful of pepper jack and allow them to melt for a minute on medium heat, right after the béchamel has thickened.

Pesto Sauce

MATERIALS
Blender

INGREDIENTS
1 ½ cups of basil
½ cup parmesan (or pecorino romano) cheese
2 cloves garlic
1 tablespoon salt
1 teaspoon pepper ¾ cup of olive oil
½ cup of walnuts
Pinch of red pepper flakes (optional)

One of my favorite lunch spots in Miami makes the best meatball mozzarella melts, which is really a mini pizza made with pita bread, sliced meatballs and a fantastic pesto sauce. This pesto sauce recipe is very traditional, and it packs a little heat. In place of pine nuts, I like to use walnuts instead because it adds a certain complexity to the dish. Besides pasta, this sauce is great as a marinade for fish and steak. In sandwiches, it can also be used to replace mayonnaise. I'll be honest here: walnuts are somewhat expensive to buy, so if you don't already have them at home, buying pesto sauce is still a good option.

5 minutes

BLEND: Combine the walnuts, cheese, red pepper flakes and basil in a blender. Blend for thirty seconds. Add the rest of the ingredients and drizzle in the oil until the sauce is smooth. Season to taste.

YIELDS ABOUT 3/4 CUP OF SAUCE

Sage Butter Sauce

MATERIALS
Blender
Microwavable bowl
Saucepan

INGREDIENTS
1 stick of butter
1 cup of cream (or whole milk)
3 tablespoons of dried sage or ¼ fresh sage leaves

Salt and pepper

This classic sauce is the perfect sauce for heartier winter pasta dishes like pumpkin and butternut squash ravioli. Impress your friends by making this ridiculously simple sauce and pairing it with store bought butternut squash ravioli (available in the frozen section for about 2-3 dollars). For a fancier dinner, serve it as a "first course", offer 3-4 pieces a person "canapé style" and blow your friends' minds.

SAUCE: Melt the butter in the microwave for 45 seconds until it is completely melted. Add the butter, cream (or milk) and sage to the blender. Blend to combine everything. If you used fresh sage, blend until the sage leaves are so small that you can't feel them when you taste (about 2 minutes). The sauce should be a light forest green color. Season with salt and pepper. Add the sauce to the pan and heat it up on medium high heat for 4 minutes, until the sauce has thickened.

NOTE: Sage can be a very strong flavor, so you don't need very much of this sauce.

Italian Sausage with Broccoli and Carrots

INGREDIENTS
3 Italian sausages
3 carrots, peeled and diced

1 yellow onion, sliced

1 head of broccoli, trimmed and blanched

Begin boiling the water in a pot.

Meanwhile in a pan, combine the sausage, carrots and onions with some olive oil and sauté on medium high for about 8 minutes or until the sausage is browned, and the carrots and onions are browned and softened. The sausage may contain extra fat which will render out, so discard it into garbage after everything has browned.

Meanwhile, trim and blanch the broccoli in the microwave.

Be sure to check the water. When it is boiling, add a large pinch of salt to the water and throw in the pasta. Every other minute, make sure you stir the pasta.

Keeping everything in the pan on medium high heat, add ½ cup of pasta water to the pan and scrape the bottom, releasing the bits that were leftover from cooking the sausage. The starchiness from the water will also help thicken the sauce. Once it comes together and has thickened slightly (about 2-3 minutes), taste and season accordingly. Drain the pasta and toss it into the carrots and sausage, add broccoli and garnish with cheese and a drizzle of olive oil. Serve.

Sweet Ham, Peas and Walnut with Pesto

INGREDIENTS
8 oz of sweet ham, whatever you like

½ cup of frozen peas

¼ cup walnut, chopped

Pesto sauce to coat (pg. 150) about ¾ cup)

Begin by boiling the pasta water.

Sauté the sweet ham and walnuts in olive oil on high heat until browned, about 3-4 minutes. Add the frozen peas, just as they are, into the pan until they are defrosted.

When the water is boiling, add a large pinch of salt to the pot and throw in the pasta. Every other minute, make sure you stir the pasta.

The liquid expelled from the peas will help deglaze the pan and create a sauce, but add ¼ cup of the pasta water to help the sauce form. Scrape the bottom and the starchiness from the pasta water will help thicken the sauce. Continue to reduce on high heat until the liquid has almost completely disappeared. Taste and season accordingly.

Throw in the drained pasta, and coat with pesto sauce. Serve with parmesan cheese.

Sautéed Eggplant and Zucchini with Cherry Tomatoes

INGREDIENTS
1 eggplant, chopped into bite size pieces
1 zucchini chopped into bite size pieces
¼ cup basil, chopped (fresh if possible)
½ cup tomato sauce (or one large ripe tomato)
4 tablespoons of olive oil
1 teaspoon of sugar

Fill a pot with water, ¾ of the way up, and bring to a boil.

Combine all the ingredients together in a pan on medium high heat and season. Sprinkle with sugar and salt- Salt is important in this case because the ingredients contain a lot of moisture. Cook until the eggplant and zucchini are fork tender, about 6-8 minutes.

When the water is boiling, add a large pinch of salt to the water and throw in the pasta. Every other minute, make sure you stir the pasta.

As the pasta is cooking, add the tomatoes to the eggplant and zucchini, and cook on medium heat just until the tomatoes start to wilt and break down.

Add the drained pasta to the sauce, and toss. Drizzle with olive oil and parmesan cheese and serve.

Rosemary Chicken Alfredo

INGREDIENTS

8 oz leftover chicken*

6 pieces of sun dried tomato, chopped (or one very ripe, medium sized tomato)

2 tablespoons olive oil

1 tablespoon rosemary

2 cloves of garlic, minced

Béchamel sauce with extra ¼ cup parmesan cheese to coat (pg. 146)

Fill a pot with water, ¾ of the way up, and bring to a boil.

Make the béchamel sauce. Follow the directions on pg. 146. When the sauce is done, add the parmesan cheese and turn the heat down to low.

When the water is boiling, add a large pinch of salt to the water and add the pasta. Every other minute, make sure you stir the pasta.

In another pan, add the chicken, garlic, tomatoes and rosemary and continue to cook on low heat until tomatoes are very soft and chicken is slightly brown. Add the drained pasta to the béchamel sauce, along with additional parmesan cheese) and taste. Makes sure everything is combined. Season again and serve.

Using raw chicken? Season it with salt, pepper and rosemary and sear on high heat for 4-5 minutes per side. Slice it and add to the sauce just before serving.

SAVE DISHES: Place the béchamel sauce in a bowl, and wipe down the pan you used to make the sauce. Use it again for the chicken.

Steak, Mushrooms and Arugula

INGREDIENTS
8 oz leftover steak, sliced thin

2 handfuls of arugula (or spinach)
½ package of mushrooms

Half an onion
1 teaspoon thyme
Extra olive oil to drizzle

Fill a pot with water, ¾ of the way up, and bring to a boil.

Meanwhile in the pan, sauté the onions, mushrooms and thyme on medium high heat; cook until the mushrooms and onions are golden brown, about 10 minutes. Season with salt and pepper.

Check the water- it should be boiling at this point. Add a large pinch of salt to the water and throw in the pasta. Every other minute, make sure you stir the pasta.

When the pasta is al dente, drain it and toss it into the pan. Turn off the heat. Add the arugula and the heat from the pasta will help wilt it slightly. Add on the sliced steak and toss again just until everything is heated through. Garnish with olive oil and parmesan cheese.

Shrimp with Bruschetta

INGREDIENTS
8 oz fresh shrimp, cleaned and deveined

2 tablespoons fresh basil (optional)

1 cup leftover bruschetta (pg. 190)

Fill a pot with water, ¾ of the way up, and bring to a boil.

Meanwhile, on medium heat, sauté shrimp until they are slightly undercooked and not completely pink, about 3 minutes. Season with salt and pepper and remove from pan and place in a cereal bowl for later.

When the water is boiling, add a large pinch of salt to the water and throw in the pasta.

When the pasta is almost ready, crank the heat up in the pan to high, and add the bruschetta. Add 1/4 cup of pasta water to the bruschetta to help loosen it and form a sauce, which should take about 3-4 minutes. Add the shrimp right before serving, and cook just until they are heated through and fully cooked. Finish with basil and parmesan.

Balsamic Glazed Scallops with Bruschetta

INGREDIENTS
8 oz fresh or frozen scallops

1 cup of leftover bruschetta (pg. 190)
2 tablespoons butter

¼ cup balsamic vinegar

Fill a pot with water, ¾ of the way up, and bring to a boil.

On medium high heat, sauté the scallops in butter. Season with salt and pepper, and cook the scallops for 3 minutes before flipping them. Cook for an additional 2 minutes on the other side. They should have a nice golden brown sear on both sides. Remove the scallops from the heat and place in a cereal bowl for later.

When the pasta water is boiling, add a large pinch of salt to the water and throw in the pasta. Every other minute, make sure you stir the pasta.

Add the balsamic vinegar to deglaze the pan, and rub off the bits from the bottom of the pan that might have settled during the cooking process. Add ½ cup of pasta water and combine with the bruschetta in the pan. Cook until the sauce is thick, about 4-5 minutes. Add the drained pasta and the scallops. Continue to cook just until the scallops are warmed through. Serve.

Sausage with Caramelized Onions, Mushrooms and Peas

INGREDIENTS

3 pieces of sausage, sliced into 1 inch pieces

Half a package of mushrooms, sliced
½ cup of peas
½ an onion, sliced

1 cup of red wine

Fill a pot with water, ¾ of the way up, and bring to a boil.

On high heat, sauté the onions and mushrooms in a pan with olive oil. Cook the mushrooms for 3 minutes before adding the salt, otherwise they won't brown. Season with pepper and cook until they are golden brown, about 5 minutes. Add the sausage and cook until everything is fully cooked and caramelized, about 5 minutes more- stir occasionally to prevent the sausage from sticking.

When the pasta water is boiling, add a large pinch of salt to the water and throw in the pasta. Make sure to stir to prevent the pasta from clumping.

Deglaze the pan with red wine and add the peas. Add ¼ cup of the pasta water and combine until the sauce is thickened and the peas are defrosted, about 5 minutes. Bring the heat down to low. Add the drained pasta and mix until everything is combined. Serve.

Bolognese Sauce

INGREDIENTS
8 oz ground beef
2 carrots, peeled and chopped
Half an onion, diced

1 tablespoon thyme
3 heaping tablespoons tomato paste

2 cloves of garlic, minced

Fill a pot with water, ¾ of the way up, and bring the water up to a boil

Dice the onions and chop the carrots.

On high heat, brown the grown beef, carrots and half an onion for 8 minutes. Season with thyme, salt and pepper. Using a spoon, drain the rendered fat into the garbage.

Add the tomato paste, minced garlic and 3/4 cup of pasta water and stir until a sauce has formed (if there is too much water, add more tomato paste, and vice-versa). Bring the heat down to medium and allow the flavors to combine. Taste and season again.

When the pasta water is boiling, add a large pinch of salt to the water and throw in the pasta. Make sure to stir to prevent the pasta from clumping.

When the pasta is al dente, drain it and add it to the pan. Toss it with the sauce for 2 minutes and finish with parmesan cheese. Serve.

This is really a meat sauce: Bolognese just sounds better.

Pasta all' Amatriciana

INGREDIENTS
Half a small white onion

1/2 cup of white wine
1 clove garlic, whole

One 12 oz can of tomato puree
Salt and pepper
3 slices of bacon

Amatriciana (A-ma-thre-chah-na) is a traditional dish from Lazio (where Rome is), but this recipe is a shortcut version of what it is because I omitted the *guanciale di maiale*, or pig cheeks (you're welcome). It is usually served with bucatini, which is a type spaghetti with a hollow center.

Fill a pot with water, ¾ of the way up, and bring to a boil.

On medium high heat, sauté the onions, bacon and garlic for 6-8 minutes until tender. Add the white wine and tomato sauce and simmer the sauce on medium heat.

When the water is boiling, add the pasta along with a large pinch of salt. Make sure to stir to prevent the pasta from clumping.

Continue to cook the sauce until the pasta is ready. When you are ready to serve, remove the garlic from the sauce and add the drained pasta. Serve with parmesan, or traditionally with Pecorino Romano.

Bacon Carbonara

INGREDIENTS
4 slices of bacon
½ cup of peas
6 oz leftover chicken
(optional)

Velouté
4 tablespoons butter
2 heaping
tablespoons flour
1/2 cup milk

1 cup of chicken
stock

The sauce for this carbonara is not traditional, because it is in fact a velouté which is a béchamel made with chicken stock. It is made in the exact same way, except you are using chicken stock in addition to milk.

Boil the water. Fill a pot with water, ¾ of the way up, and bring up the heat to high.

Brown the bacon on medium high heat until it is crispy. Season with pepper and drain on a plate lined with a paper towel. Discard the extra fat.

Meanwhile, add the pasta to the boiling water and season with salt. Cook until the pasta al dente, and then strain.

Make the velouté in the same manner you would make the béchamel (see pg. 146). When it is finished, add parmesan cheese, peas and the rest of the bacon.

Toss with pasta and serve with parmesan cheese.

Mexican Pasta

INGREDIENTS
8 oz leftover taco meat (or chicken)
3 slices of bacon (optional)

Béchamel sauce to coat, with ½ cup of melted cheddar (See pg. 148)
1 cup of canned salsa

Fresh parsley (garnish)

Boil the water. Fill a pot with water, ¾ of the way up, and crank the heat up to high. On a paper towel lined plate, microwave the bacon for 3 minutes.

In the pan, make the béchamel sauce (see pg 146). When it is done, add the salsa, cheddar cheese and the leftover taco meat to the sauce. Combine everything together until heated through, and keep warm on medium low heat.

Meanwhile, add the pasta to the boiling water and season with salt. Cook until the pasta is al dente, and then strain.

When the pasta is cooked, add it to the pan. Combine all the ingredients together (don't forget the bacon) with the nacho cheese béchamel sauce and serve.

Shrimp with Asparagus, Cherry Tomatoes and Basil

INGREDIENTS
8 oz of shrimp
A handful of asparagus, trimmed and cut into bite size pieces
Package of cherry tomatoes
1 tablespoon basil (fresh or dried)
Salt and pepper

Fill a pot with water, ¾ of the way up, and bring the water up to a boil.

Microwave blanch the asparagus (pg. 222). Throw some ice into it afterwards to prevent it from overcooking. Toss the shrimp and cherry tomatoes into the pan and season with salt and pepper. Cook until the tomatoes are wilted and have popped, and the shrimp are completely pink, about 4 minutes. Turn off the heat and remove the pan off the burner.

Meanwhile, add the pasta to the boiling water and season with salt. Cook until al dente, and then strain.

When you are ready to combine everything, heat up the pan to medium. Add asparagus and the drained pasta. Toss together until everything is combined, and season with basil. Finish with a drizzle of olive oil.

Bacon with Tomatoes and Cream

INGREDIENTS
4 strips of bacon
1/3 cup cream

1 small can of
tomato paste
1 tablespoon thyme

1 teaspoon red
pepper flakes
(optional but
recommended)

The first time I tried this pasta was at the Ristorante Ferrari during a summer abroad program in Perugia, Italy. Served with gnochetti (mini gnocchi), it was incredibly satisfying and rich for something as simple as it was to make. Pancetta and bacon are both interchangeable in this recipe; simply remember to drain the grease out of the pan before adding the tomato sauce and cream.

In a large pot, boil water on high heat. Once the water is boiling, add the pasta and a large pinch of salt, and cook until the pasta is al dente.

Meanwhile (as the water is boiling), microwave the bacon on a paper towel lined plate for 4 minutes. In a sauce pan on medium heat, combine 3 heaping tablespoons of tomato paste and 1/3 cup of cream. Stir until the tomato paste has completely dissolved and the sauce is thick and pink, about 6 minutes. If the sauce is too thick, add an additional tablespoon of cream. Add the bacon, thyme and red pepper flakes and simmer it on low heat until you are ready to add the pasta.

Toss the pasta with the sauce and combine until everything is coated. Finish with parmesan and serve.

PASTA RECOMMENDATION: Gnocchi.

Frutti Di Mare

INGREDIENTS
6 oz of clams, washed
6 oz of mussels, washed
8 cherry tomatoes or 1 medium size
tomato (as ripe as possible), chopped
3 tablespoons fresh basil, chopped
4 tablespoons olive oil
Salt and pepper
2 cloves garlic, minced
½ cup white wine (optional, but highly recommended)

The best frutti di mare that I have ever had was on the island of Capri, off the coast of Naples. The seafood was unbelievably fresh, even though the waiter was a stronzo who bit my head off when I asked for cheese for my pasta.

"Non lo so, ma a-soma people will a-kill- you for uh-asking for thee- cheeZe-on-the-pasta"*.

WHAT HAPPENED TO THE CUSTOMER IS ALWAYS RIGHT!

The best time to eat shellfish is anytime except the summer. Even though shellfish is available year round, the general consensus is to eat shellfish with months that have R's in them (see pg. 279 for explanation). Don't worry though, it's not *NECESSARILY* true. Buy whatever is available at the time, and you only need about a 12-16 oz of shellfish for two servings.

Boil the water by filling the pot ¾ of the way and cranking the heat up to high.

In a pan on medium high heat, add the olive

oil, garlic, clams and the mussels

with the white wine and tomatoes. Season with salt and pepper. Cover and cook for 6 minutes, just until the clams and mussels have started to open up. Turn off and cover with a lid on and the heat and the mussels and clams will continue to cook.

Meanwhile, add the pasta to the boiling water. Throw in some salt to season the water. Cook until the pasta is al dente, about 10 minutes. Drain.

On medium heat, add the cooked pasta to the pan and toss everything together. The heat from the pasta will help continue to cook the mussels and clams.

Continue to stir everything together until the mussels and clams have opened completely (about a minute more because most should have already opened at this point). Discard any ones that have remained shut.

Garnish the dish with fresh basil, a drizzle of olive oil and serve with CHEESE!

TIP: You can buy an assorted variety of shellfish in the freezer aisle of some grocery stores.

*I don't care about the rules. I only wanted to put cheese on the pasta.

Tuscan Pesto

MATERIALS
1 blender

INGREDIENTS
1 package store bought fresh basil
2 oz of sundried tomatoes

1 1/3 cup of olive oil
¾ cup of pine nuts
(toasting is optional)

In Italy, there are great programs called agriturismo where a local producer or family will make visitors a typical regional meal. The first one I went to was right outside of Sienna, and I didn't really pace myself as I should have. I ended up drinking 1 1/2 bottles of wine, 3 espressos as well as half our table's worth of food. I couldn't move for about 16 hours. Despite the circumstances, I still remember this pesto as the best I ever had.

Boil the water. Fill a pot with water, ¾ of the way up.

In the sauce pan, add the pine nuts and allow them to toast on high heat for about 5 minutes. They should start to get dark brown on the outside.

Add the toasted pine nuts, basil, sundried tomatoes and olive oil to the blender and give it a whirl. Blend it until the sauce forms a thick sauce.

When the pasta water is boiling, add the pasta and cook until the pasta is ready and al dente, about 10 minutes. Drain the pasta.

In the same sauce pan, add the drained pasta (with about ¼ cup of leftover pasta water) and the pesto sauce. Stir until the pasta is coated and the sauce has slightly thinned. Serve hot or cold.

PASTA RECOMMENDATION: Mini penne.

Rigatoni with Artichokes and Peas

MATERIALS
One plate lined with paper towels

INGREDIENTS
One 14 oz can of artichokes
3 strips of bacon (optional for Vegetarians)
1 1/2 cup of low sodium chicken (or vegetable) stock
1/2 cup of frozen peas
2 cloves of garlic (optional)
pepper
2 tablespoons of butter
1 tablespoon dried basil

Fill a pot with water, ¾ of the way up and bring up the heat to high.

Microwave the bacon for 3 minutes until brown and crispy.

Over the sink, drain the artichokes. In a pan on medium high heat, cook the artichokes and garlic for 7 minutes with ¾ cup of chicken broth, until the liquid has evaporated.

When the pasta water is boiling, season with salt and add the pasta.

BLEND: In the blender, add the rest of the chicken broth along with the artichokes and garlic and blend until you are left with a smooth puree. Add the contents back to the pan, along with the frozen peas. Add the butter, basil and pepper and taste. Adjust the seasoning if necessary. Keep the sauce warm on low heat. It should be thick.

Drain the pasta when it is finished and toss it into the sauce. Stir until everything is thoroughly combined. Serve with parmesan cheese.

PASTA RECOMMENDATION: Rigatoni

Above: Sausage with caramelized onions, mushrooms and peas. Below: Rigatoni with artichokes and peas.

SANDWICHES

VARIATIONS ON THE SANDWICH

- HAM

Prosciutto is a fantastic ham from the Emilio Romagna region in Italy. The city from where the most famous prosciutto is made is Parma, the same region famous for its milk (*Parmalat*) and cheese (*Parmesan*). At first taste, prosciutto may seem salty, but it is a very versatile ingredient and can be featured in a sandwich, wrapped around a piece of melon or with a breadstick. Because prosciutto can be kind of pricey, it can be substituted with **Serrano** ham, a cheaper, similar tasting ham from Spain.

There are a lot of great hams available on the market, like sundried tomato and rosemary and Parmesan crusted, to even classic honey maple. You can also try **pepperoni**, **salami**, the best being from Genoa, and **chorizo**, a spicy Spanish sausage.

- CHEESE

When you consume cheese, it releases an opiate as it digests, which explains why it is literally addictive. As a result, it's beneficial that most cheeses are expensive (because they are imported), but if you are willing to spend a little more on good cheese, there are hundreds of great varieties available. Some of my favorite snacking cheeses are **manchego** (which is Spanish), **brie** and **chevre** (goat cheese), which may be an acquired taste. When looking for a sandwich cheese, look for a great melting one, like **gruyere**, **jarlsberg**, **havarti**, **provolone** (which is really aged **mozzarella**) and **muenster**. I wouldn't recommend adding **blue cheese** to any sandwich unless you really like blue cheese and are eating it in a steak sandwich because it can overpower the ingredients.

- BREAD

Try deviating from regular, pre-sliced bread because after a while it gets pretty boring. Today, there are lots of great options available in supermarkets. My favorite ones to use for sandwiches are French **baguette**, **ciabatta, Cuban bread** rolls and **croissants**. For those of you are looking for great options beyond bread, try using **pita** and **English** muffins (which not only toast up well, but also don't get soggy-perfect for burgers). **Wraps** and **tortillas** also round out the bread substitutes.

- SAUCE

For a healthier option, try using **pesto** instead of **mayo.** I know a lot of people like mustard and mayonnaise and I'm not trying to convince you not to use them, but try substitutes like **hummus** which add both flavor and act as a binder. A vast majority of students will go to a sandwich shops like Subway with a healthy lunch in mind, and will eat more calories than they would have regularly because of condiments like mayonnaise and other fatty dressings. In its place, try using pesto or goat cheese if you are a fan of it.

- RUB THE BREAD WITH GARLIC

Although it may seem like a really odd ingredient to have in a sandwich, a simple rub of garlic on warm bread will create an entirely new flavor, without running the risk of chomping on raw garlic. Simply peel the garlic and toast the bread. While the bread is warm, take the whole clove of garlic and rub it across the sandwich.

Combinations:
- Turkey BLT with pesto
- Leftover steak, brie, arugula on toasted English muffin
- Grilled cheese with bacon
- Chorizo and manchego
- Prosciutto (or Serrano) ham with fresh mozzarella and basil

Appetizers

Fried Green Tomatoes

MATERIALS
Nonstick pan
Tongs
Cereal bowl
Spoon, fork, or
whisk

Plate lined with
paper towels

INGREDIENTS
¾ cup of oil
1 large green tomato
1/2 cup flour

1/2 cup of cold
water, plus 2
tablespoons
1 tablespoon paprika
1 teaspoon dried
basil (optional)
Salt and pepper

The first time I ever tried fried green tomatoes was at Gladys Knights Fried Chicken and Waffles in downtown Atlanta. It's possible that I was born in the wrong part of the south because I began obsessing with the deliciously crispy and sweet tomato with spicy pepper sauce days after I had eaten it. After a number of trials, I found that a tempura battered tomato crusted with panko resulted in the crispiest texture, but because that was too time consuming, I tried it with a basic tempura batter and found it was just as good.

15 minutes

BATTER UP: In a cereal bowl, combine the flour with the spices. Slowly pour in the cold water and continue to stir until a batter forms. Don't worry if you can't get out all the lumps, but try your best. You may not need all the water- stop until the batter is smooth and thicker than a cake batter. It should be light red in color if you added paprika.

SLICE: Cut the green tomato into slices that are about 1/3 of an inch in size. It should be about the width of a Burger King hamburger patty. Try and keep the slices about the same size so they finish cooking at the same time.

FRY: In the pan, heat up the oil on high heat. To check if the oil it hot enough, throw a little bit of the batter into the pan. It should begin to sizzle and puff up- if it sinks to the bottom, then the oil isn't hot enough, and if starts to splatter, then the oil is too hot.

Coat the tomatoes in the batter until they are completely

color. To test the doneness, spear a tomato with a fork. If it goes in easily, then it is done.

Drain the tomatoes onto the plate and keep warm in the oven at 200 degrees until you are ready to serve.

MAKES 2-3 SERVINGS

covered and place them into the pan. It's important that you don't crowd the pan, and if your pan is about 10-12 inches in diameter, about three tomato slices should be enough for your first batch.

Once you put them in the pan, they should start to sizzle immediately. LOWER THE HEAT TO MEDIUM.

TRY: Try it with a spicy pepper oil.

Cook for about 3 minutes on each side, and then flip. You will know they are ready to flip because they underside of them will begin to form a golden crust.

Once they are flipped, cook for an additional 2 minutes on the other side. They should be golden brown in

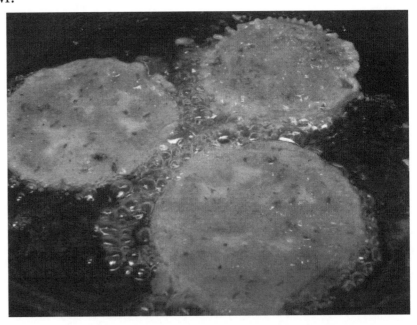

Bacon Wrapped Cherry Tomatoes

MATERIALS
1 baking sheet
Tongs
Toothpicks
Cutting board
Chef's knife

INGREDIENTS
1 package of cherry tomatoes (about 20)
7 strips of bacon
2 tablespoons of olive oil

Salt and pepper
*I use about 1 strip of bacon for every 3 tomatoes

Bacon wrapped cherry tomatoes are really great appetizers that are simple to make and very impressive. The crunchiness of the bacon works wonders with the sweetness of the cherry tomatoes. Make a lot of these because your friends will eat them like m&ms.

15 minutes

PREP: Preheat the oven to 400 degrees.

Wash and clean the cherry tomatoes, removing the leaves and anything else that's inedible.

On the cutting board, slice each of the pieces of bacon into 3 pieces.

Wrap one piece of bacon around the cherry tomato, and secure both ends of the bacon with the toothpick. Continue until all the tomatoes are complete.

ROAST: Place the tomatoes and bacon on the baking sheet and toss with olive oil, which will prevent the tomatoes from sticking. Season everything with salt and pepper. Roast for 10-12 minutes. The bacon should be crispy and the tomatoes should be slightly wrinkled. They will release a lot of moisture so you may want to set them onto a plate lined with paper towels before serving. Serve hot.

MAKES ENOUGH FOR 6 PEOPLE

Angelie's Egg Rolls

MATERIALS
Non stick pan
Cutting board (to roll)
Small bowl of water
Kitchen tongs
Chef's knife
Large microwavable bowl

INGREDIENTS
1 pound chicken breast, shredded (use leftovers, optional)
1 medium onion, chopped
3 cloves of garlic, minced
1 package of frozen mixed vegetables (like cauliflower, broccoli, carrot)
1 cup frozen corn
1 cup frozen peas
2 packages of spring roll pastry (thawed)
½ cup soy sauce
1 tablespoon pepper
1 cup chicken broth
2 cups of vegetable oil (to fry)

This may be the most time consuming of all the dishes featured in this book, but I guarantee you that you will fall in love with these eggrolls. By using frozen vegetables, you also cut the prep time in half.

These eggrolls store very well in the freezer and all you need to do is defrost them for a couple seconds in the microwave before frying them.

DEPENDS ON HOW MANY YOU MAKE minutes

Begin by defrosting the spring roll pastry. You can do it in the microwave, or if you do it the day before, just leave it in the fridge.

PREP: Chop the onions and mince the garlic. Meanwhile, place all the frozen vegetables in a large microwavable bowl and add 1/2 cup of water. Heat for two minutes until everything is defrosted. Discard the excess liquid.

SAUTE: Add all the vegetables to the pan (except the chicken, which you can add at the end). Add the soy sauce, the pepper and the chicken broth and continue to cook on high for about 10 minutes, until all liquid has evaporated. Add the remaining chicken and stir just until everything is evenly distributed.

ROLL: See the following page for step by step instruction.

FRY: Rinse out the sauce pan with some water and dry it with a kitchen towel. On high heat, add the oil. When the oil is hot, add the eggrolls. Cook until light brown, about 2 minutes and flip. Continue to cook for another two minutes until it is completely brown all around it. Drain them on a plate lined with paper towel and keep them warm in the oven. Serve with Thai chili sauce (or sweet and sour sauce) for dipping.

To roll the eggrolls: Begin by separating the pastry. Add the filling to the bottom corner, and fold over the rest of the edges. The eggroll should now resemble step four. Carefully, roll up the base of the eggroll to the tip. Use your finger, and brush some water across the edge before you seal, which will keep the eggroll intact. Fry.

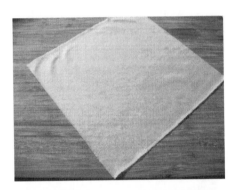

Tia Les' Fire House Chicken Wings

MATERIALS
Baking sheet
Spatula

INGREDIENTS
5 pounds chicken wings
1 package Italian dressing seasoning (buy in the grocery store, not zesty) per tray

A couple tablespoons of honey
Cooking spray
2 teaspoons cayenne (optional)
Salt and pepper

I came by this recipe from my aunt, and loved it so much that I began to request it for birthdays. When I was a swimmer, I could eat thirty of these without breaking a sweat, and even though they are simple, they are perfect for parties because they can be made in batches of twenty pounds as easily as batches of two pounds. Use cayenne pepper to really wake your guests up, but offer an option and only season half of them with it.

45 minutes

TO COOK: Preheat the oven to 350 degrees. Spray the cookie sheet. Align the chicken wings on a baking sheet, leaving a little room to separate the wings. Season the wings with Italian dressing, and cayenne if preferred. Cook the chicken wings for 25 minutes. Carefully drain the oil into a bowl and turn chicken wings. Re-season the other side of chicken wings. Cook for another 15 minutes. Drizzle with honey during last ten minutes. Serve either hot or at room temperature.

MAKES ABOUT 30 WINGS

NOTE: Do not drizzle with honey too early otherwise the sugar in the honey will cause the wings to burn.

Guacamole

MATERIALS
1 Cutting board
1 large bowl
Chef's knife
1 spoon

INGREDIENTS
1 large ripe avocado
¼ cup of finely minced red onion (about a quarter of an onion)

Salt and pepper
Two lemons, juiced
1 small jalapeno pepper, finely diced (for heat, optional)

If you've ever been to a Mexican restaurant and seen waiters make guacamole at the table, you've probably noticed how easy it is to make. All you really have to do is throw everything in a bowl, stir and mush. The trick to keeping the avocados green is to add something acidic to them, like lemon juice. Guacamole is also traditionally made with cilantro, but I hate it, so I omitted it from this recipe. Make sure you season and taste and re-season this recipe!

10 minutes

PREP: Open the avocado. If you have never opened an avocado before it's very easy. Split the avocado lengthwise with your knife. You'll notice you won't be able to cut through because of the pit, so use your knife to slice around the whole fruit. When you're done, you'll be able to pull apart the avocado and remove the pit.

Using your spoon, trace around the rim of the avocado, pulling the fruit away from skin. Once you have circled the entire avocado, place the spoon into the underside of the flesh and dump it into the bowl. Discard the skin and repeat with the other half.

Chop the red onion (and jalapeno if you like) and squeeze the lemon juice into the bowl. Season everything with salt and pepper and then mash it up together, making sure everything is thoroughly combined. I like chunky avocado, but feel free to make it however you like.

NOTE: The heat of the chili is both in the membrane and the seeds. If you really like spice, try using a Serrano chili- but they are pretty hot.

Datiles con Beicon

<u>MATERIALS</u>
Nonstick pan
Cutting board
Knife
Tongs

Toothpicks (one for each date that you make)
Plate lined with paper towels

<u>INGREDIENTS</u>
1 package of dates (pitted)
1 package of bacon
1 cup of vegetable oil
Salt and pepper

A traditional Spanish tapas dish, datiles con beicon are usually stuffed with marcona almonds (a type of Spanish almond) and blue cheese. For this recipe, all you need is a package of dates (the best are *medjool* dates, but any large date will work) and a package of bacon, maybe a couple of drinks and you're having a great night.

10 minutes

PREP: Cut each bacon slice into thirds (or in half, depending on how much bacon you want). Place the date horizontally into each piece of bacon and roll it up. Secure the bacon to the date with the toothpick, inserting it so that it goes through both ends of the bacon. Don't worry if the ends of the date aren't covered with bacon.

FRY: Heat up the oil on high. When you place your hand six inches above the pan and can feel the heat, add the dates. If you are making a lot, cook the dates in batches. *If you add it all at once, you will crowd the pan and the oil will drop and the dates will become greasy and less crispy.* For a 9 inch skillet, add about 8 at a time.

As soon as you add the dates, immediately lower heat to medium. Fry for 2-3 minutes on one side, turn and continue for another minute. Remove the dates from the pan and drain the dates on the paper towel. Season with salt and pepper and eat!

FEEDS 4-6 PEOPLE

Shrimp with Garlic Oil

MATERIALS
Non stick pan
Wooden spoon
Chopping board
Chef's Knife

INGREDIENTS
1 ½ pounds of
shrimp, peeled and
deveined
1 ½ cups of olive oil
10 cloves of garlic

3 tablespoons parsley
1 tablespoon paprika
2 lemons (or limes)
juiced
Salt and pepper

The first time I ever had this dish was when I visited Madrid, Spain. Even though it is landlocked, Madrid has one of the highest consumption rates of seafood in the world, so everywhere you look, you can get seafood in little pastries or atop pizza. This shrimp dish is extremely easy to make and can feed a lot of people with very little effort.

12 minutes

PREP: This may seem tedious, but trust me, it makes a difference. All you have to do is get the shrimp and split them in half lengthwise (along where the digestive tract would be). You'll be left with two thinner pieces of shrimp that are mirror images of each other. Remember that the smaller the item is, the faster it cooks, so you are actually saving time by doing this. (PS It's also a restaurant trick- restaurants will cut shrimp in half so they can make twice as many dishes, and people will think they're eating the same amount of food). Season the shrimp with paprika, salt and pepper.

Meanwhile, chop the garlic and the parsley. Using the back of your knife, press against the garlic and the pressure should cause the skin to pop right off. Chop the garlic into a couple pieces, but don't worry if any of them are big because all we really want is for their flavor to infuse into the oil. We're not going to actually eat them.

SAUTE: In the pan on medium high heat, combine the oil and garlic. All we want is the flavor of the garlic to infuse, but we don't want it to brown. If it gets too dark, lower the heat. Cook for 3 minutes and then increase the heat up to high for 1 minute before adding the shrimp.

Add the shrimp and sauté for 1 and a half minutes. Then remove the pan off the heat. They will continue to cook. When they are done, they should have curled unto themselves and be pink in color. Squeeze the lemon/lime juice onto the shrimp, season with salt and pepper and finish with the parsley. Serve with toothpicks.

SERVES 6-8 PEOPLE

Above: Datiles con beicon. Below: Salt and pepper shrimp.

Salt and Pepper Shrimp

MATERIALS
Nonstick pan
Wooden spoon

INGREDIENTS
1 pound shrimp, peeled and deveined
1 teaspoon salt
1 teaspoon pepper
2 tablespoons oil
1 teaspoon sesame oil (optional, but this is the secret)

Every time my grandma has a dinner at her house, I greet her first and the shrimp second. The best thing is that this recipe only requires 3 ingredients. Serve these hot, or at room temperature, or use the shrimp on top of the Asian Pizza [see pg 197]. The secret to this recipe is the sesame oil. You don't need to buy the dark sesame oil called Kampari (and to be honest, I've never even used it). The cheap one works the best!

8 minutes

SAUTE: On medium high heat, allow the oil to heat up for about a minute. Add the shrimp and season with salt and pepper. Cook for five minutes, or until the shrimp are pink, soft and tender. Remember the shrimp will continue to cook even after they are out of the pan, so it's better to undercook them than overcook them.

Drizzle the sesame oil over and stir so all the shrimp are slightly coated. *Sesame oil is very strong so you don't need that much.* Serve.

MAKES 6-8 SERVINGS

Bruschetta

MATERIALS
1 cutting board
1 knife
1 baking sheet

INGREDIENTS
1 loaf of Italian ciabatta or French baguette
6 tablespoons olive oil
Cooking spray
3 cloves garlic, peeled
5 medium size vine ripe tomatoes*
2 tablespoons balsamic vinegar
3 tablespoons of sugar
6 large fresh basil leaves, or about 1 and 1/2 tablespoon dried basil
¼ cup Parmesan cheese (garnish)
Salt and pepper

Bruschetta is perhaps one of the most identifiable of the Italian antipasti. Strangely enough, it refers not to the topping, but to the thickness of bread. Thicker slices of toasted or grilled bread are bruschette (singular bruschetta), thinner slices are crostini (crostino).

The pronunciation is also sometimes confusing. In Italian, the c-h-e sounds like que, which would be pronounced brus-quet-ta. Every time I go to a party, people kill this in about 30 minutes, so trust me, this recipe is better than anything you can buy at the store.

10 minutes

PREP THE BREAD: Preheat oven to 400 degrees. Slice the bread into thick slices, about ¾ of an inch in thickness. Coat the pan with cooking spray to prevent sticking.

Place the bread on the baking sheet and drizzle with 2 tablespoons olive oil. Toast the bread for about 5 minutes, until it is slightly browned. For garlic lovers, use one clove of peeled garlic and rub the tops of the bread. The heat from the bread will cause the garlic flavor to infuse into the surface, without having to chop garlic into the mixture.

Garnish with parmesan cheese and serve alongside the tomato topping.

FOR TOMATOES: Dice tomatoes into about ½ inch cubes and places inside bowl. Chiffonade basil (cut into strips) and mince garlic into fine pieces. Combine with tomato, sugar, olive oil and balsamic vinegar. Season liberally with salt and pepper. Taste and add more sugar if necessary. Store it in refrigerator. This mixture is best made up to two days ahead. Allow it to come to room temperature before serving, as the oil will solidify when chilled.

YIELDS ABOUT 3 CUPS OF TOMATOES

TIPS: Use the best tomatoes available, which peak during the summer months but can be available year round. Avoid plum tomatoes if you can because they really don't taste like anything. Cherry or grape tomatoes make excellent substitutes because of their sweetness, but are usually more expensive. Simply cut them in half or into quarters.

TRY: For a quick meal, combine tomato topping with pasta and sprinkle with cheese. For a quick side dish, make Summer Corn Salad. Serve with tacos or as a topper to salad.

Summer Corn Salad

MATERIALS
Microwavable bowl
Spoon

INGREDIENTS
Leftover Bruschetta topping (pg. 190)
Frozen corn
Frozen peas

2 tablespoons water
salt and pepper
1 tablespoon of butter

This summer corn salad is so named because I first made it during the summer, even though everything was from the frozen section of the grocery store. You can also add canned, drained black beans and salsa instead of bruschetta and call it a *southwestern corn salad*. The ratio for this recipe should be equal parts of all three elements.

5 minutes

BRING TOGETHER: Combine frozen corn and peas in a microwavable bowl. Add the water and cook in microwave for 2 minutes on regular setting. Drain the remaining water and add the tomato topping. The heat from the corn and peas should warm up the topping, and the mixture should smell of tomatoes, garlic and basil. Add the butter until it melts. Season to taste.

IMPRESS: Add thinly sliced carrots to the mixture. Sauté it with butter and 1 tablespoon of sugar until tender.

Sautéed Sweet Corn

MATERIALS
1 nonstick pan
Wooden spoon
Microwavable bowl

INGREDIENTS
8 oz of frozen corn (you can buy a 1 lb. bag and keep it in the freezer)

2 tablespoons sugar
Pinch of salt
2 tablespoon of butter

My friend Lauren has family in Virginia, and while I was over at her house one day force-feeding the entire dessert section, her mom told me a story about her own mom's cooking.

Whenever they went to visit Virginia, Lauren's grandma would make a deliciously sweet sautéed squash dish that no matter how hard they tried, never turned out the same way at home. At first they thought it was the vegetables, that the squash in Miami wasn't sweet enough, so they bought different varieties. And then they tried adjusting the seasoning and the way they were cooking it, but it still wasn't the same.

Finally one year, they finally asked for the secret, and Lauren's mom passed the secret on to me.

"Honey, just put a little sugar on it."

So I did, and I have to tell you, it works on everything.

For this recipe, you can use both frozen and fresh corn. Try making it on the grill as well, with some butter and sugar to give it a nice caramel color.

6 minutes

SAUTE: On medium high heat, add the butter and corn to the pan (you don't need to let it melt). Add the sugar and mix everything so that the corn is coated with the sugar. All we're really trying to do is dissolve the sugar and slightly brown the corn.

Cook the mixture for 5 minutes. The corn should be slightly darker in color and the outside should be shinier. Season with salt and serve hot.

MAKES 2-3 SERVINGS

Garlic Bread

MATERIALS
Microwavable bowl
Baking sheet
Tablespoon
Cutting board
Chef's knife

INGREDIENTS
1 loaf of French bread
5 cloves of garlic, finely minced
¾ stick of butter

Salt and pepper
1 tablespoon dried basil
1 teaspoon dried oregano (optional)
Cooking spray

Garlic bread is fantastic way to get people to stop talking.

Use a French baguette for this method of preparation as it will absorb the most liquid without getting mushy. Garlic bread can be very messy, so if you prefer a more refined approach, simply create the dipping sauce using olive oil instead of butter and add a few drops of balsamic vinegar. Serve on a shallow plate, or individual salad plates if you want to impress your significant other's parents.

15 minutes

Preheat the oven to 350 degrees.

PREP: Finely mince the garlic and combine it with the butter in the microwavable bowl. Microwave on regular power for 1 minute until the butter is completely melted. Set aside to cool and season with salt, pepper, basil and oregano.

While the butter and garlic are melting, make one inch slits into the French baguette, cutting ¾ of the way down, just shy of cutting all the way through- keeping the baguette whole will expedite the cooking process and make clean up easier. Spoon the garlic butter into the slits of the baguette, until all pieces are moistened. A little bit will do, maybe half a teaspoon's worth per cut. You may have some leftover sauce. Bake it in the oven for 10 to 15 minutes, or until the baguette is brown and crusty. Eat!

MAKES 6 SERVINGS

Butter vs. Olive oil

Butter and olive oil serve the same general purpose in many countries but they have very different properties. Butter has a lower heat resistance than olive oil, and will brown once it passes its heat threshold. Typically, many recipes combine the two when sautéing vegetables to utilize both the flavor of the butter and the high temperature resistance of the olive oil.

Butter, when allowed to melt and cool, will separate into different layers of fat and oil. Restaurants chefs usually will skim the top layer of butterfat and discard it, leaving something called **clarified butter**, which has the flavor of butter with a much higher cooking temperature. I've never done this before because it's too time consuming for the average home cook.

Butter may not be as bad for you as you think. In an article from Bon Appétit Magazine, Nina Planck differentiated the health risks between butter and butter substitutes. Trans fats found in margarine increase an individual's LDL cholesterol levels, which are bad for you, and lower an individual's HDL cholesterol levels, which are good. According to a Harvard professor cited in the interview, over 100,000 premature deaths have been linked to this cause. Unfortunately, the FDA links natural and synthesized saturated fats, which confuses the consumer as to what is really good for you. So my advice is this: eat butter, its better!

Parts of Italy, home to some of the highest percentages of centegenerians in the world (people over 100 years old), have been using olive oil as a life source for centuries. Extra Virgin olive oil is considered the main cooking staple for Mediterranean cooking and it is widely available at affordable prices. Singers sometimes drink olive oil to help with their voices, and according to my mother, it's supposedly also good for your skin.

Baked Pita Chips

MATERIALS
A small baking sheet
cutting board
Knife

8 minutes

INGREDIENTS
1 package store
bought pita bread
1 tablespoon oregano
1 teaspoon garlic
powder
1 tablespoon of
pepper
2 tablespoons of
olive oil

Preheat the oven to low broil (or about 400 degrees) and cut the pita bread into triangles. Pour enough olive oil on baking sheet to coat it.

Toss the pita bread and drizzle an additional tablespoon of oil over it. Season everything with oregano, garlic powder, salt and pepper, and bake for about 5-7 minutes until the pita are crispy but not browned. Serve warm.

Asian Pizza

MATERIALS
1 baking sheet
1 knife
1 cutting board
1 tablespoon

INGREDIENTS
1 store bought pizza dough (available in the dairy aisle)
1 thinly sliced carrot
1 head of broccoli
¾ cup of Asian dressing (such as sesame- ginger, or peanut)

10 oz chicken (see Chicken Milanese recipe)
1 package of crispy Chinese noodles (optional)
16 oz package of mozzarella cheese

The first time I made this pizza, I created it out of desperation. I was having a dinner with fifty hungry guests, and the deep fried butternut squash ravioli had already run out. So, scrambling around the tiny kitchen where I was manning the food preparations, I found leftover Asian dressing, carrots, broccoli, chicken tenderloin and pizza dough. Almost instantly, the Asian pizza was created. This is a great opportunity to use leftover chicken and any vegetables that you like.

20 minutes

Preheat the oven to pizza dough as high as it can go, at least 450 degrees.

Spray the baking sheet with cooking spray or oil the pan to prevent the dough from sticking.

Spread out the dough to desired thickness. *I recommend a thicker dough because the toppings are heavy.*

BAKE: With a tablespoon, pour Asian dressing and spread along entire pizza dough. Cover the pizza with chicken, carrots, broccoli and mozzarella cheese.

Cook the pizza. (Be advised that pizza can be cooked at the highest temperature possible in your oven, usually 500 degree Fahrenheit) for 8-12 minutes. The cheese should be melted and crust should be browned along the edges. Allow the pizza to cool slightly before serving, about 5 minutes, otherwise it will be hard to slice.

Sprinkle with crispy Chinese noodles and serve immediately.

MAKES 1 LARGE PIZZA

LEFTOVERS: There won' be any, but eat it for breakfast the next day.

LEFTOVER DOUGH: Make a *foccacia*, which is Italian style bread. Roll it into long pieces, drizzle it with olive oil, and season it with salt and rosemary. See the dessert section for other ideas.

IMPRESS: Sprinkle with sesame seeds and toasted peanuts.

Macaroni and Cheese

MATERIALS
1 pot
1 pan
1 wooden spoon
1 strainer

INGREDIENTS
1 pound elbow macaroni (or whatever you like)
1 recipe of béchamel sauce (pg. 148)
One 8 oz package of cheese (buy the blend)
1/2 cup sour cream
1 teaspoon each of Salt and pepper
4 slices of crispy bacon (optional)

Stop buying mac and cheese from a box! This recipe will teach you how to make an awesome mac and cheese in the same amount of time and for less money.
Some of the best restaurants in the world even offer their own version of mac and cheese, like The French Laundry's Lobster and Orzo mac and cheese. This recipe for macaroni and cheese can easily be stretched for more people and for a cheaper price that the box in terms of servings. Plus it's freaking amazing.

15 minutes

FOR THE PASTA: Fill up the pot and bring water to a boil. Season the water with a tablespoon of salt and add the pasta. (Optional: lay the bacon on microwavable plate and cook for four minutes until it is crispy. Allow it to cool and break into small pieces with your fingers).

FINISH: While the water is boiling, make the béchamel sauce (pg. 148). (Melt the butter and flour together to make a roux, and add the milk. Cook until the sauce is thick.) When the sauce is finished, add the cheddar cheese and sour cream and melt together until everything is combined. Season with salt and pepper, and add the bacon. Once the pasta is cooked (about 10 minutes), drain thoroughly and toss it into the mixture until pasta is completely coated. Serve immediately.

MAKES 6 LARGE SERVINGS

TRY: Baking the macaroni and cheese. Preheat the oven to 350 degrees. Using an oven-safe pan or dish, add pasta and cover with an additional 1 cup of cheese. Cook for 20-25 minutes until cheese is melted and browned.

IMPRESS: Add white cheese instead of yellow cheese to béchamel, and toss in cooked shrimp, sundried tomato and basil. Cover in cheese, toss over enough Panko bread crumbs on top for some crunch. Bake for 30 minutes at 350 degrees. Garnish with truffle oil.

Nachos

MATERIALS
1 microwavable bowl
1 microwavable plate
1 oven safe plate
1 cutting board
1 knife

INGREDIENTS
8 oz leftover chicken or steak, cut into bite size pieces
1 large bag of favorite tortilla chips, such as Tostitos
1 cup sour cream, divided into two
1 cup guacamole (optional)
1 cup cheddar cheese
2 tablespoons of milk
Salt and pepper
1 cup salsa
4 strips bacon (optional)

Nachos are the quintessential snack for drinking nights, so you really don't want to mess around with them. It also is a great way to get rid of leftovers. Simple nachos just have cheese on them, but take the opportunity to clear your fridge of everything you don't want. Cover it in the cheese sauce and serve it to your drunk friends.

10 minutes

FOR THE CHIPS: Preheat the oven to 200 degrees. Open the bag of Tostitos and place them on the oven safe plate. Add the leftover chicken or steak, making sure they are cut into bite size pieces. Keep the plate in the oven, allowing them to warm, until you are ready to serve them.

Meanwhile, in the microwave, cook the bacon for 4 minutes or until brown and crispy. Set aside to cool.

In the microwave again, add sour cream, cheddar cheese and milk and stir together until reasonably combined. Season with salt and pepper. Cook for 1 minute, and stir again. Cook for additional minute if necessary, or until the mixture is hot. The cheese sauce should be completely melted and thick, but not burned. If the cheese sauce still hasn't achieved the right consistency, continue to cook in 30 second intervals. Add an additional tablespoon of milk if it becomes too thick.

TO COMPLETE: Right when you are about to serve, remove the nachos from the oven and spoon over the cheese sauce so that it covers everything. Crumble the bacon on top. Spoon over the remaining guacamole, salsa and sour cream around the edge of the plate and on top of the nachos. Serve immediately.

MAKES 1 BIG PLATTER OF NACHOES

IMPRESS: Add some heat. Place a minced jalapeno into the cheese sauce while it cooks in the microwave. Your friends will immediately fall out of their drunken stupors.

Fried Ravioli

MATERIALS
Non stick pan
Kitchen tongs
Cereal bowl
Fork or spoon
Plate lined with
paper towels

INGREDIENTS
A 1 lb package of
frozen ravioli
1 tablespoon paprika
Salt and pepper
1 tablespoon oregano
1 tablespoon basil
½ cup parmesan
cheese (to garnish),
optional but
recommended)

½ cup of tomato
sauce (jarred tomato
sauce is fine)
1 ½ cup of oil

Tempura Batter

1 cup flour
1 and 1/2 cup of cold
water, with 2
additional
tablespoons

When I was studying abroad in Italy, I was so tired of eating pasta day after day that I wanted to strangle myself with a fettuccine. But late one night while my friends and I were making dinner, I decided to try and fry up some ravioli. They liked them so much that I found myself becoming Italy's Taco Bell, trying to satisfy late night cravings. The trick to these ravioli is, once again, the tempura batter. Use any type of ravioli you like, but I think the hands down favorite is still the basic cheese.

15 minutes

ALLOW: The ravioli to defrost in the microwave or at room temperature for 5-10 minutes for minimal splattering while cooking. The liquid from the defrosted ravioli will react with the hot oil, so be very mindful to let them COMPLETELY defrost.

BATTER UP: Make the tempura batter. In the cereal bowl, combine the flour with the paprika and oregano. Slowly pour in the cold water and continue to stir until a batter forms. Don't worry if you can't get out all the lumps, but try your best. You may not use all the water- stop until the batter is about as thick as a cake batter. It will be light pink from the paprika.

FRY: On high heat, add the oil to the sauce pan and allow it to heat up. Test the oil with a bit of the batter. It should sizzle, but it shouldn't sink. If it sinks, the oil is too low; if it splatters, then the oil is too hot.

Coat the ravioli and add them to the pan. They should begin sizzling. Cook for about 3 minutes on each side. *The ravioli typically will puff up in the center, but don't worry. Try not to puncture the holes, otherwise the filling will expel into the oil and make a huge mess.*

Continue to fry and flip. When they are golden brown, set them on the plate or keep them warm in the oven at 200 degrees. Garnish them with cheese and serve them with tomato sauce to dip in.

DESSERTS

3 Minute Hot Chocolate, Hot Chocolate Cake

MATERIALS
1 microwavable mug
1 spoon
1 small plate
1 bowl

INGREDIENTS
1 package hot chocolate mix (SWISS MISS)
3 tablespoons oil
3 tablespoons of milk
Pinch of salt
2 tablespoons flour
2 tablespoons sugar
1 egg

Peanut Butter Sauce
¼ cup smooth peanut butter
1 tablespoon milk

As I was looking through my pantry for microwavable recipes, I noticed my leftover hot chocolate mix and it suddenly dawned on me: wouldn't it be cool if I could make a chocolate cake in the microwave, from hot chocolate mix?! A lot of my friends living in dorms may not have all the right spices, but they definitely had hot cocoa mix. Eight different variations later, I had an amazing midnight snack.

3 minutes

COMBINE: Place everything in a mug and stir until everything is completely incorporated. Be careful with the egg because you don't want to have lumps.

MICROWAVE: Cook for 1 minute and 30 seconds for a soufflé like texture, and 2 minutes for a denser cake.

SAUCE: Combine the peanut butter and milk in the bowl. Microwave for a minute, or until the peanut butter is loosened. Drizzle on top of the chocolate cake. Serve with ice cream.

MAKES 1 SERVING

Fried Oreos

MATERIALS
1 nonstick pan
1 bowl
1 spoon
1 spatula (or tongs)

INGREDIENTS
Tempura batter
1/2 cups flour
1 pinch of salt
3/4 cup of ice water, with additional 2 tablespoons

8 Oreos (or how many it takes to clean out the tempura batter, frozen for at least 10 minutes)
1 Tablespoon of cinnamon (optional)
1 cup oil

This was one of the messiest recipes to test, but towards the end, I found myself and my guinea pigs licking everything that remotely resembled the cookies, like door knobs and car tires.

The trick to frying Oreos is to make sure that the oil is hot and the Oreos are cold. In Japanese restaurants, menu items like fried ice cream and fried cheesecake are first frozen solid then deep fried very quickly. The heat is just enough to partially melt the inside. All three of these items start with a basic tempura batter.

10 minutes (plus at least 15 minutes to freeze oreos)

ASSEMBLE: In the bowl, combine flour, cinnamon and salt to begin the tempura batter. Using the spoon, stir continuously while adding the ice water. The thickness of the tempura should be around the same as a cake batter, and should adhere well to the outside of the Oreos.

FRY: Heat the oil in a sauce pan on high heat. You want the oil to be hot, but not deadly hot. *Test the oil by dropping a pea size amount of batter into the pan: if it falls to the bottom, the oil is too cold and if it starts to pop, then the oil is too hot. You want the batter to sizzle gently and float to the top.*

Fry the Oreos for 1 ½ minutes then flip. Be careful not to touch the Oreos before otherwise it will get stuck to the bottom of the pan. *If they stick, gentle insert the spatula under the each cookie and carefully slide it off the bottom..* As soon as you flip, turn off the heat.

Keep the Oreos in the pan for 1 minute, until they are golden brown. The outside should be crispy and the inside should be soft. If you froze the Oreos before hand, the inside will be harder. Drain and serve immediately.

MAKES 2-3 SERVINGS

IMPRESS: Serve with melted peanut butter or nutella dipping sauce (pg. 32), and with vanilla ice cream.

Nutella Pizza

MATERIALS
1 baking sheet
Cutting board
1 knife
2 microwavable bowls

INGREDIENTS
1 can of store bought pizza dough, or equal amount of fresh pizza dough (you can buy both at the grocery store)
½ package of frozen blackberries (or whatever berry is cheapest)
1 cup cashews (hazelnuts, pecans or walnuts) chopped
2 tablespoons sugar
1 ½ tablespoons cinnamon
2 tablespoons of milk
1 cup of nutella sauce (pg. 32)

I created this pizza recipe for a large dinner party, just hoping to use up some extra pizza dough. This pizza can be substituted with anything seasonal, but frozen fruits like blackberries, raspberries and strawberries work perfectly.

20 Minutes

ASSEMBLE: Preheat the oven to 400 degrees, or according to the package directions. Bake the crust for 8 minutes or until it's browned and fully cooked.

In a microwavable bowl, combine the blackberries and 2 tablespoons of water. Cook for 2 minutes, or until the blackberries have cooked down so it's syrupy, but there are still pieces of blackberries throughout. If necessary, continue to cook, checking every minute.

In the other microwavable bowl, melt the cup of nutella and milk for a 1 min. and 15 seconds, or until the nutella is soft enough to pour. Sprinkle the entire pizza crust with cinnamon sugar. Add the chopped nuts and blackberries so that it is evenly distributed across the pizza and drizzle the nutella. Serve immediately with some ice cream.

MAKES 4-5 SERVINGS

Chocolate Apples

MATERIALS
1 pot
Wooden spoon
Forks
Parchment paper, or aluminum foil sprayed with cooking spray

INGREDIENTS
8 oz chocolate chips (use both bittersweet and semi-sweet if you can, you don't need milk chocolate because we will be adding cream later.)
4 granny smith apples

1 stick of butter
1 cup of roasted peanuts, chopped
1/2 cup cream
1 tablespoon salt
2 tablespoons of leftover brewed coffee (optional)

People always think of county fairs when they think of candied apples, but the truth is that they are really easy to make (albeit a little messy). The best time to make these is in the fall when apples are at their peak. Try and find granny smith apples (or red delicious) because they will hold their shape the best without getting soggy. If you are serving this for a fondue night, slice the pieces of apple and let your friends dip them into the sauce afterward.

10 Minutes

CHOCOLATE SAUCE: This is called a *ganache*, which is a French term meaning chocolate and cream. The *ganache* forms the base for a lot of desserts.

On medium low heat, add the chocolate chips, butter and coffee to the pot, and allow the chocolate to melt, stirring regularly; *chocolate burns easily so I know this is annoying on low heat, but just let it sit there for 5 minutes.* Once it is melted, add the cream and salt. Cook for 5 minutes, allowing the cream to help thicken the chocolate. Once the mixture is thick enough so that it resembles a very thick syrup, you're ready to dip.

TO DIP: Using the forks, spear the apple so that you have a solid hold onto it. Place the apple in the pot and swirl it around until it is completely covered in chocolate. Place the spoon vertically so that the excess chocolate dribbles away without ruining the outside. Set aside to cool temporarily and continue with the next apple.

These apples must be double dipped- Dip them again and repeat the same process. While they are still warm, cover them with toasted peanuts and allow them to cool for at least 15 minutes in the fridge. Serve cold or at room temperature.

MAKES 4 SERVINGS

NOTE: Most chefs recommend to use bark chocolate instead of chocolate chips because the chocolate chips have been chemically altered to retain their shape. But who cares? They aren't going to taste any different and bark chocolate is expensive.

EVOLUTION AND IMPRESS: Use leftover ganache and make **truffles**! Place the ganache in the fridge and allow it to harden for 1 hour. When it has hardened, spoon out some of the ganache and roll it into a ball with your fingers and set it on aluminum foil so it won't stick. Place them back in the fridge to harden some more, and remove 10 minutes before you are ready to serve.

Pizza Dough Cinnamon Rolls

MATERIALS
1 baking sheet
Spatula
Aluminum foil

INGREDIENTS
1 package of pizza dough (really you don't need a whole package, so if you have leftover dough that's just as good)
3 tablespoons sugar
2 teaspoon cinnamon
6 oz chocolate chips
6 oz walnuts, chopped (optional)
Cooking spray

I've never met anyone who didn't like cinnamon rolls, or at the very least, who couldn't see the appeal cinnamon rolls had to everyone else.

There are many great cinnamon roll recipes out there, many of which require making your own dough etc and many great varieties that you can buy pre made in the store.

This recipe had a very practical purpose. I had one package of pizza dough and I wanted to see how many recipes I could get out of them. The first time I made this recipe, I used leftover trail mix as my filling.

25 minutes

Preheat the oven to 350 degrees.

PREP: Chop the walnuts into smaller pieces. It doesn't have to be perfect so don't sweat it.

ASSEMBLE: Roll out the pizza dough and spray it with cooking spray. Sprinkle the whole mess with the cinnamon and sugar so that every bite is coated. Add the chocolate chips and walnuts in the same manner, making sure that every bite is covered.

Carefully, roll the dough. I roll it lengthwise (meaning I start folding along the longer side) so that the dough yields more cinnamon rolls. Pull the ends from the dough and gradually lay it upon itself. Just do it slowly and work your way up, making sure to keep the dough the same thickness throughout the entire log.

When you have a long cylindrical piece of dough, you can start cutting. Make cuts that are about 1 inch wide because they will puff up in the oven.

BAKE: Line the baking sheet with aluminum foil and place the rolls on top, leaving a couple inches in between them so they have room to puff up. Sprinkle them with some more cinnamon sugar and cook for 15-18 minutes, until they are golden brown. Serve hot or with store bought vanilla icing.

MAKES 6-8 SERVINGS

Chocolate Dipped Strawberries

MATERIALS
Pot
Wooden spoon
Parchment paper, or aluminum foil sprayed with cooking spray

INGREDIENTS
8 oz chocolate chips (use both bittersweet and semi-sweet if you can, you don't need milk chocolate because we will be adding cream later.)

1 package of strawberries, washed
1/2 cup cream
1 stick of butter
1 tablespoon salt
2 tablespoons of leftover brewed coffee (optional)

When I was 12 years old, I went with my family to San Francisco for the first time. We were headed to Alcatraz when we stopped at Fisherman's Warf for a snack, and at a small farmer's market, I found strawberries the size of my fist and a cup of chocolate sauce for dipping. I was so excited I didn't realize until I went to buy them that the crazy vendor wanted $20 for the strawberries. Jerk!

On the ferry ride over, we obliterated the package in less the 5 minutes and put on a show for the other passengers at the same time. When we finally arrived at Alcatraz, my sister, cousin and I were still licking our fingers, and with no napkins in sight, appeared like we had just swam up Willy Wonka's chocolate river.

15 minutes, plus chilling time

CHOCOLATE SAUCE: We are making a *ganache*, which is a French term meaning chocolate and cream.

On medium low heat, add the chocolate chips and butter to the pot and allow them to melt; chocolate burns easily so I know this is annoying on low heat, but just let it sit there for 5 minutes. Once it is nearly melted, add the cream and salt. Continue to cook for 3-5 minutes, allowing the cream to help thicken the chocolate. Once the mixture is thick enough so that it resembles a very thick syrup, you're ready to dip.

TO DIP: Drop the strawberries into the chocolate sauce, and allow the excess chocolate to drip off. Place the strawberries on the parchment paper or aluminum foil and allow the chocolate to harden. Repeat until all the strawberries have been coated and allow them to sit for about 15 minutes.

Repeat the process. The strawberries are best double-dipped. When all the strawberries have been recoated, allow them to harden in the fridge until you are ready to eat. Serve cold or at room temperature.

SERVES 4-6 PEOPLE

Fried Doughnuts

MATERIALS
1 nonstick pan
Kitchen tongs
Plate lined with paper towels

INGREDIENTS
Leftover pizza dough (it doesn't matter how much you have)

2 tablespoons sugar
1 teaspoon cinnamon
1 cup vegetable oil

This was the second recipe I made with the canned pizza dough. Pizza dough is so ubiquitous that it was only a matter of time before someone just threw it into hot oil and fried it up. Finish it with cinnamon sugar and some chocolate syrup and you got a great dessert in less than 10 minutes.

PREP: Rip the dough into pieces. It doesn't matter how big they are. If you are aiming at uniformity, use the edge of a glass and make circles with rim.

FRY: In the nonstick pan, add the oil and bring the heat up to medium. Test the dough to see if it's hot enough by adding a pea size amount of batter. It should sizzle gently and float up to the top. *You don't want the dough to be as hot as you would use for frying meat, because then the dough will burn on the outside and be raw on the inside.*

When the oil is heated, add the dough. All we are doing is browning the outside because the dough will cook quickly. It should puff up almost immediately. It's important to turn the dough every once in a while so it doesn't get too dark in any place.

Fry for about 3-4 minutes total, constantly moving the dough around. When the dough is golden brown, remove and allow them to dry on the paper towels. While they are still hot, sprinkle the fried dough with cinnamon and sugar. Serve hot.

Left: Frozen hot chocolate. Below: Fried donuts with chocolate sauce.

Frozen Hot Chocolate

MATERIALS
1 blender
1 mug

INGREDIENTS
1 package of hot chocolate, or 1/3 cup of leftover melted chocolate ganache
1/2 cup of water (or milk if using ganache)
Hit of cinnamon
Hit of cayenne (optional)
Small pinch of salt
½ cup of crushed ice
Whip cream

On the Upper East Side of Manhattan, there is a small restaurant built into the crevice of two other buildings called Serendipity's. It's the same place from the movie with Kate Beckinsale and John Cusack. I went there in the middle of the night with a friend, and we gorged ourselves with their famous frozen hot chocolate and 300 pound chocolate cake. Here is a recreation of their famous hot chocolate.

8 minutes

MICROWAVE: The first thing that is necessary is to dissolve the mix or ganache into the liquid. Follow the directions from the package, or combine the ganache with milk. Microwave (or stir if using ganache) until thoroughly combined. Season it with salt and cinnamon or cayenne and place it in the freezer for 10 minutes.

BLEND: When the chocolate is cold, place it into the blender. Add ice until it starts to thicken like a milkshake. When it is thick and the ice is blended through, dollop with whip cream and enjoy.

MAKES 2 SERVINGS

TECHNIQUES

Microwave Blanching

MATERIALS
Chef's knife
Cutting board

Cereal bowl
INGREDIENTS
Water

Salt
Ice
Vegetables, trimmed

Blanching is a form of cooking vegetables just long enough until they are tender and vibrant in color. After trimming down vegetables, one usually blanches them by throwing them into a large pot of boiling water for a second just until they are tender, and then quickly into a bowl of ice water so that they maintain their color and don't overcook.

Traditional blanching requires too many steps and dishes, so here are the basic directions for blanching vegetables in the microwave. This technique should be used with fresh vegetables like broccoli, cauliflower, string beans and edamame- the method will brighten the flavor and the vegetables will still maintain their shape and color.

3 minutes

MICROWAVE: Fill up the bowl three quarters of the way full with water. Wash and trim the vegetables, and place them in water. Season them with salt and microwave on regular power for 2 minutes, or until they are softened but still tender. If the vegetables are still firm, add 30 seconds, but it should be no more than 3 minutes. *They should be greener in color but continue to hold their shape.*

Carefully drain the hot water from the cereal bowl. Throw in some ice and add a quarter cup of cold water back into the bowl with the vegetables and allow it to cool. Once cooled, drain and set aside until you are ready to cook or serve. Finish by adding the vegetables to a salad or sautéing them in a pan with butter.

TIP: The same method works with frozen vegetables. *I would recommend only using corn, green beans, peas, and lima beans from the frozen section, as some other ingredients like broccoli are too soft in their frozen form.* To 'blanch' frozen vegetables, simply add several tablespoons of water to cereal bowl and add vegetables. The frozen vegetables will defrost and the liquid will be released. Cook for 1 1/2 minutes. Add ice to the bowl and allow them to cool before draining.

Roasting

MATERIALS
MATERIALS
Cutting board
Knife
Baking sheet

INGREDIENTS
Vegetables, sliced into uniform pieces
Olive oil
Salt and Pepper

Roasting is an extremely simple way to amplify the flavor of any vegetable, and it really changes the identity of an entire dish. When roasting vegetables, a typical rule of thumb is the "fork rule". Simply stick a fork in the vegetables, and if they are soft (but not too soft that they are falling apart), then they are done.

The best way to guarantee perfectly roasted vegetables is to chop all the ingredients into the same size. Also, coat everything generously with salt and pepper, as the salt extracts the moisture from the vegetable and will concentrate the flavor. Try this with anything, especially asparagus, mushrooms, fennel, butternut squash, potatoes and sweet potatoes, cherry tomatoes and carrots.

Depends on which vegetables you are using-minutes

Preheat the oven to 400 degrees. Convection roasting also works well in this case.

Wash and trim the vegetables. Oil the baking sheet liberally and add the vegetables. Season everything with salt and pepper and toss together.

Roast until the vegetables are soft and fork tender. The vegetables should a 'tanned' and covered in brown marks. Be sure to move them around every 10 minutes or so, as the sugar from the vegetables (like carrots, cherry tomatoes and sweet potatoes) will be released and will make the vegetable stick to the pan.

IMPRESS: Roast potatoes and sweet potatoes with whole cloves of garlic. Garlic will sweeten and will be taste fantastic by itself, but if you like, you can throw it out or mince it before serving.

Combine leftover roasted vegetables with milk, cream, water, or chicken stock in the blender for a great soup. Blend until vegetables reach desired texture, adding extra water or stock to thicken as needed. Reheat it in the microwave or sauce pan and serve. Freeze your leftovers when you're done.

TIPS: When roasted, mushrooms and eggplant will release a lot of liquid because they are very porous. Make sure to discard liquid every 15 minutes, otherwise the vegetables will steam and not roast.

Knife Skills and Chopping

Basic knife skills are essential to any beginning cook- some chefs even argue that the way different vegetables are cut will change the way they taste.

BUYING: When purchasing a knife, find one that you feels comfortable in your hand. While many professional chefs use longer knives, I wouldn't suggest anything longer than about 7 inches for a beginner. Opt for a classic chef's knife, instead of a cleaver. *The one I own is a 7 inch santoku style knife by a German company called Wusthof*, but there are many great choices available for less than 20 dollars. Go to Marshalls for a great selection.

GRIPPING: The knife should become an extension of your hand. Grip the knife by the handle, and position your thumb and index finger around the sides of the blade. If you are right handed, your thumb should press against the left side and the index finger on the right. The last three fingers should grip the underside of the knife and provide the stability.

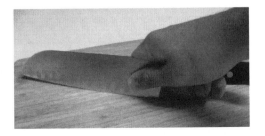

CREATE FRICTION: When slicing anything, the best way to start is to create a flat, stable surface. If

Remember to use the knife as a wedge instead of a saw. When chopping, the tip of the knife should stay planted on the board, and the only part that should move is the bottom. When slicing, use the tip of the knife as a guide, and make long strokes down the fruit or vegetable. And don't rush; we're not in a competition here.

you are chopping on a slippery tabletop, place a thick placemat (or something that will create friction) under the cutting board and this will prevent it from sliding. When slicing round vegetables, it is always easier to cut on a flat surface- simply trim off an edge from the vegetable, and the vegetables won't slide from under your fingers.

Most importantly, CURL YOUR FINGERS! As long as you have curled fingers along with a good grip of the vegetable, you won't cut yourself or slice your fingers off.

CHOPPING VOCAB

SLICING: I usually use two different techniques for slicing, depending on the vegetable I'm using.

For circular vegetables like carrots or cucumbers, slicing just means making thin circular discs. Simply make a shallow, lengthwise cut into one side of the vegetable so that you have a relatively flat surface and make you're thin slices.

The second method of slicing is used for things like French fries, zucchini, or anything

that requires long strips of vegetables. Begin by peeling the vegetable, if necessary, and make another shallow cut to create your flat surface. Cut lengthwise so you are left with long strips.

DICING: The term dicing (in this book) usually refers to an ONION, because it has a very specific method of chopping. Any other vegetable can simply be chopped roughly, but if you practice dicing the onion as shown (pg. 233), you can cut through it in less than thirty seconds, and you won't be left crying after.

MINCING: Mincing means a very small chop (less than 1/8 inch long pieces), and usually refers to GARLIC.

TRIM: Trimming means removing the stalk and any other inedible parts of the vegetable, like the tips of green beans or the broccoli core.

EXTRA CREDIT: These terms aren't used in this book, but are frequently used in other books.

CHIFFONADE: A French term that describes a method of chopping that enables you to chop large amounts of fresh herbs (particularly basil) very quickly. All you need to do is take a couple leaves of whatever you are trying to chiffonade, and stack them on top of each other. Then, carefully, roll them up like you would resemble a little cigar. When everything is rolled up, begin making thin slices into the leaves. When you are done, you'll be left with long, thin strands of the herb.

JULIENNE: Another French term describing an occasionally impractical method of chopping that is only really necessary for a couple of different recipes. It is essentially chopping vegetables so that they resemble match sticks.

Broccoli

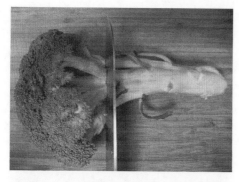

Use this technique for cauliflower as well.

To trim the broccoli, cut into the highest part of the stalk to separate it from the head of the broccoli. Discard the stalk.

You can now see the broccoli segments on the head: simply continue to make shallow slices along the segments to divide it into bite size pieces.

If you have any additional stalk remaining after you have separated the segments, trim it off and discard as well.

The broccoli can now be microwave blanched or roasted.

Only buy fresh broccoli- frozen broccoli is too soft after it is defrosted.

String Beans

String beans are also called haricot verts.

Begin by lining the string beans in a row. Do this stage in groups of ten beans to simplify the process.

Align the beans on their left so that their ends are at the same level. Make one long slice and to remove the ends.

Do the same for the right side. Align the beans so their tips are level, and make another long slice.

Repeat the process until all of the beans are trimmed.

The string beans are now prepped.

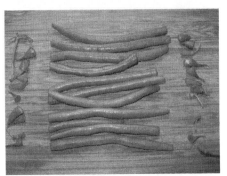

Tomatoes

Use this technique with other circular fruits and vegetables, like eggplant and peaches. Always cut off a piece of an edge to ensure that you have a flat surface.

To remove the core, think about cutting out a triangle. Slice the tomato in half. Make a shallow, diagonal cut around into the left side of the core and another diagonal cut into the right. The core should resemble a triangle and remove easily.

To slice, halve the tomato and simply make long, smooth strokes.

To dice, stack 2-3 slices on top of each other. Slice parallel strips into the tomato, and then make perpendicular slices in the other direction. It should look like a checkerboard.

Asparagus

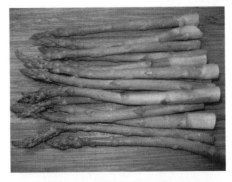

The time of year will determine how big the asparagus are.

Asparagus have tender ends that tell you where they should be cut, usually in the bottom two inches. Take one feel towards the end. Then snap the asparagus and discard the end.

Align the asparagus up by their tips. They're all relatively equal in length, so they should all snap in about the same area.

Using the first asparagus as a standard, make a slice into all of the asparagus to remove their ends.

Now they can be roasted and sautéed.

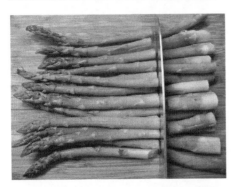

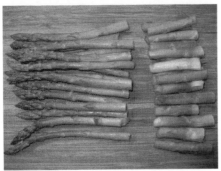

Onions

At first, this method may seem unnecessary and difficult. However, if you practice, you'll be able to chop an onion in less than 30 seconds.

To counteract the crying, put on swimming goggles or freeze the onions beforehand.

Slice off the two cores at either end of the onion, and then cut the onion lengthwise (you'll be splitting down the core into two pieces).

To dice, follow the lines along the onions and make long slices about 1/8 of an inch thick, being careful not to slice all the way through the onion. You want to keep them in one piece for the later steps.

Onions II

*After you have made the shallow slices, carefully make horizontal cuts **into** the onion that are perpendicular to the original slices. Also remember not to cut all the way through. (see the picture for assistance)*

After this step, all you have to do is turn the onion and slice down against your original slices. You will be left with small, uniform pieces.

***To slice**, refer back to the 3rd picture of pg. 233. Instead of slicing into the onion, slice down horizontally so that your cuts are perpendicular to the lines on the onion. Your cuts will look like half moons, but the pieces will pull apart from each other while cooking.*

Carrots

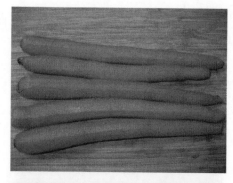

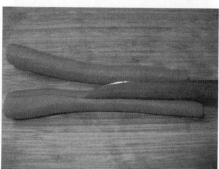

This method can also apply to parsnips, although I doubt anyone is going to use them.

Carrots are the worst vegetables to cut because they have such an unusual shape. When you are cutting them, it is important to remember to find a flat surface and to curl your fingers.

Begin by peeling the carrots. If you are using them in a stew, don't worry about it being perfect.

Align the carrots by their ends, and slice them off. Realign them by their tips and slice them off as well.

Slice each of the carrots in half lengthwise, so that you are left with 4 pieces, each with a flat surface.

Carrots II

Further slice the carrots in half, so that the carrot yields 8 long pieces. In this case, use your knife as a wedge and it will guide you on where to cut.

After you have 8 pieces of carrots, simply line them up together. Making long, smooth slices with your knife, cut along the edge of the carrots so that you are left with small pieces. This method enables you to chop carrots into whatever size you want.

Potatoes

z

Potatoes don't need to be chopped perfectly because regardless of their shape, they are going to be eaten.

Begin by peeling the potato. Split it in half so that you are left with a flat surface.

*For a **rough chop**, cut the potato into three large strips. Then make perpendicular cuts into the potato, so that it resembles a checkerboard. (See picture 3 and 4.)*

To slice a potato in circular discs, cut off an edge of the potato to make a flat surface. All you have left to do is make narrow slices into it, resulting in pieces about the size of large poker chips.

Potatoes II

To the left: a roughly chopped potato.

*For a **finely chopped** potato, begin by creating a flat surface. Cut the potato lengthwise so that you have long, thin pieces (See picture 2 on this page).*

Stack 1-2 pieces of the long pieces and follow the same idea behind the rough chop. You want to try and make your slices and cross-slices thinner.

***French fries**? If you are crazy enough to make French fries, refer to the second picture on this page. After you have long thin pieces, all you need is to slice thin strips into them and you're done.*

Themed Nights

Use the following ingredients to transform some of your dishes

- Spanish- paprika, cumin, red pepper flakes, bell peppers, onions, garlic, black beans, chick peas, lime, lemon, parsley
- Mexican- cilantro, bell peppers, chipotle, salsa, red onions, corn tortillas, black beans, dark chocolate, chilies
- Italian- basil, oregano, pepper, olive oil, tomatoes, balsamic vinegar, parmesan cheese, prosciutto ham, garlic, flat leaf parsley, rosemary
- Indian- turmeric, fennel seed, cumin, nutmeg, masala, coriander
- French- herbs de Provence (thyme, basil, fennel seed, marjoram, lavender), butter, salt, pepper,
- Greek- oregano, garlic, lemon, pistachio, olive oil, rosemary, pita, lamb
- German- beer, potatoes, sauerkraut, pretzels
- Japanese- panko bread crumbs, fresh seafood, sticky rice, soy sauce, teriyaki sauce, seaweed, edamame, sesame seeds, sesame oil, ponzu, wasabi, tofu, sriracha
- Thai- Thai chilies, spicy chili sauce, panko bread crumbs, hot pepper paste

LEFTOVER ALCOHOL

- Vodka- tomato sauce with cream- vodka sauce
- Rum- banana, brown sugar, vanilla ice cream (bananas foster)
- Orange flavored liquor (Grand Marnier, Triplesec, Cointreau)- chocolate cake, French toast batter.
- Beer- Beer with brats, beef stew, beer batter

GOURMET CORNER

GOURMET CORNER

I wrote this gourmet section for more experienced cooks, and I wanted it to be the section I would have enjoyed if I had been seeing this book for the first time. Many of these recipes were developed over time: innovations from classic recipes, things I picked up while I was travelling or recreations of some of my favorite meals from various restaurants. These are recipes you want to pull out if you're trying to impress someone, but they were still written with the average college student in mind.

This section features real restaurant quality food. Some of these recipes may take a longer time to make than the previous recipes, and might include some pricier ingredients but it is still cheaper and more impressive than going out to eat.

At first glance, these recipes may seem to more difficult than the others, but I want to dispel that idea right now. They are written longer in order to give you a detailed description of every step. Cooking is all about confidence, so just take it one step at a time, and you'll have a fantastic meal that people will remember in no time.

IMPROVING YOUR COOKING

To be a great cook is more about only buying the best ingredients or spending hours behind a stove. A great cook knows who he or she is cooking for and transforms a simple meal into something memorable.

Kitchen experience is important, so I'm not saying you'll be able to butter poach a lobster or make a soufflé; however, here are a few key ideas anyone can use to transform their food overnight.

- SALT IN STAGES AND DON'T BE SKIMPY.

Many people have very decisive stands on where salt comes into play with your meal, but every single chef worth his salt (sorry, I've been waiting 200 pages to write that) will tell you that it is probably the single most important ingredient available. When you cook, salt every stage of production. If you are broiling or grilling meat, the salt should cover nearly every single part of the meat; and when you are making pasta, you not only need to salt to pasta water, but the sauce as well.

REMEMBER: *Don't go overboard because you can always adjust the seasoning later. All that all you need to make anything taste better is a pinch of salt at a time, or about ½ teaspoon.* Don't wait until the last minute to salt otherwise your food will just taste salty.

- TASTE AS YOU GO.

This may seem like a really rudimentary idea, but it is singlehandedly *the biggest mistake novice chefs make when it comes to preparing food*. If you don't taste as you're cooking, the flavor will intensify, so not only will it taste bad but it will taste worse the longer it cooks. Taste a sauce halfway and adjust it if necessary, but always taste it before you are going to serve it.

- LESS SAUCE, MORE FLAVOR.

In theory, this point goes hand in hand with the addition of salt because salt acts as a natural dehydrator. But if you are making a sauce for a steak, take the time to reduce it and you will have a more intense, richer flavor than if you were simply serve it as is.

This idea applies to pasta sauces as well, but only up to a certain point. With pasta sauces, you want enough sauce so that it clings to the pasta. In the same respect, you want that sauce to be thick and velvety, so take the time to reduce as well, but only partially.

- ADD A PINCH OF SUGAR TO FRUIT AND SOME VEGETABLES

Fruits and vegetables at their peak of ripeness are always much sweeter than if you were to buy them normally. So mimic the ripeness by adding some sugar to them! All fruits will benefit from the addition, as well as some vegetables like carrots, all types of squash, zucchini, sweet potato and even tomato bruschetta (pg. 190).

- MY HEIRARCHY OF TASTES: CRUNCHY, SALTY, SWEET, SOUR AND BITTER

From personal experience, I've noticed that people tend to prefer the first three, and avoid the last two. Cook for your audience.

- BUTTER

We are all French in some ways. Finish sauces, vegetables and almost whatever you like with a pat of butter, and it will be like you've never eaten the dish before.

Cream of Mushroom Soup

MATERIALS
1 large pot
Cutting board
Chef's knife
Wooden spoon
Blender

INGREDIENTS
2 pounds of mushrooms (anything you like, but I like cremini)
½ cup dry red wine
2/3 cup cream
2 cloves of garlic, whole
3 Tablespoons butter
½ cup milk
Salt and pepper
2 tablespoons olive oil
2 teaspoon dried rosemary (or one fresh sprig)

I was about 13 years old the first time I ever tried making mushroom soup, and I had just finished watching Wolfgang Puck's television show. He had just made an amazing wild mushroom soup that I was determined to reproduce. I remember it took my sister 30 minutes to clean about 2 pounds of mushrooms, and as payback, I ended up taking almost 2 hours to make a 45 minute recipe. But after some trial and error and a few years of hard work, I figured out a way to make it without any effort at all. Serve this with crunchy French bread.

40 minutes

PREP: Take the skins off of the garlic by applying pressure to the garlic with the side of your knife and pressing down.

Slice the mushrooms into smaller pieces, but it doesn't need to be perfect because we're going to blend them anyways.

SAUTE: In the pot, add the butter and olive oil. *We combine them because we want the flavor of butter, but the higher cooking temperature of olive oil.* Add the whole pieces of garlic, the mushrooms and the rosemary.

Allow the mushrooms to cook where they are and resist the urge to toss them around in the pan too much because you want them to get brown. Cook them for

8-10 minutes *before* seasoning them with salt and pepper.

The mushroom will release a lot of moisture (with the help of the salt) so allow them to cook until the moisture evaporates. This will take an additional 10 minutes, but it will depend on what type of mushroom you are using.

When the liquid has evaporated, deglaze the pan with the wine and scrape off any bits that might have settled on the bottom. Continue to cook the mushrooms for an additional 5 minutes or until the wine has reduced in volume by half. If you used fresh rosemary, remove the stem from the pan.

BLEND: Place the mushrooms and milk into the blender and blend until the mushrooms are completely smooth. (I also like my mushroom soup very smooth, but if you like it with a little texture, don't puree it all the way).

HEAT BACK UP: Place the mushroom puree back into the pan and add the cream. Bring the heat back up to medium high heat and cook for 3-5 minutes, just until it is heated through and the cream has thickened the soup. You'll know when it's done because the mixture will be very thick and coat the spoon.

Lower the heat to low and simmer for 10 more minutes, so that the flavors combine. Season with salt and pepper, taste and serve.

MAKES 6 SERVINGS

Curried Carrot Soup

MATERIALS
1 large pot
Cutting board
Chef's knife
Wooden spoon
Blender

INGREDIENTS
1 package of carrots (about a pound)
1 1/2 cup of water
1/3 cup sugar
2 tablespoons butter
2 small (or 1 medium) potatoes, peeled and diced
Salt and pepper
2 cloves garlic, peeled
2 tablespoons of curry powder
1/2 teaspoon cinnamon (optional)
¾ cup sour cream

Thanks to The French Laundry Cookbook, one of the best lessons I ever learned about food is that food should taste like the best version of itself. Soup really takes that idea to the next level: it extracts the flavor, concentrates it and makes a vegetable so much better than it really is.

Different vegetables are enhanced through different cooking approaches; carrots, which have so much natural sweetness, are best glazed because glazing highlights their natural sweetness.

In this recipe, potatoes are used because their starchiness serves as a natural thickener, and they prevent the soup from becoming too sweet.

30 minutes

PREP: Roughly chop the carrots and the potatoes: you don't have to chop them perfectly, but you want to chop them into small pieces because the smaller they are, the faster they'll cook (the same idea applies to the potatoes). You don't want to put anything in the blender that's not completely soft because it won't blend.

Peel the garlic by applying pressure to the garlic with the side of your knife- it should fall right off.

GLAZE: Glazing is a really easy cooking method that a lot of people really overlook. Simply add 2 cups of water to the pan, and add the carrots and sugar, garlic and potatoes. Cook on high for 10 minutes, stirring occasionally but you don't really need to do much of anything. All you really want to do is to evaporate the water and soften the carrots and potatoes. Use the edge of your spoon and push down on the carrots: they should be very soft that they almost break apart. If they still aren't soft, add an additional 1 cup of water and cook until that evaporates as well. When you are done, you should have very soft vegetables and about ½ cup of water left in the pan (this will help you blend).

BLEND: Add the carrots, potatoes and the remaining water into the blender and puree until smooth.

POT: Add the puree back to the pot and season with curry powder, cinnamon, salt and pepper. Add the sour cream and stir until combined. Finish with the butter and stir just until the butter is melted. Taste and re-season if necessary. Serve hot.

IMPRESS: This is a pretty rich soup, so you really don't need that much of it. If you're looking to be fancy serve it in a small dish with a slice of toasted French bread laid across and a dollop of sour cream in the center.

MAKES 4 SERVINGS

Roasted Tomato Soup

INGREDIENTS

1 large pot
1 baking sheet
Chef's knife
Cutting board
A blender
1 bowl

INGREDIENTS

1 28 oz can tomato puree
3 cloves garlic
1 small onion
1 package of fresh basil, chopped
1 cup cream
2 tablespoons olive oil
Salt and pepper

As far as I know, I had the best lunch system in Florida, if not the United States. My school lunch was Cuban influenced, but on those rare days of American patriotism, there was nothing better than their cream of tomato soup, which I would drink in 20 oz Styrofoam cups by the barrel.

This recipe can be made a couple different ways, but all you really need is a 28 oz can of tomato puree, some seasoning and cream, and you're done.

30 minutes

PREP: Chop the onions and fresh basil. Smash the garlic cloves to remove the skin, but keep them intact.

SAUTE: On medium high heat, add the oil, onions and garlic to the pan. Allow them to cook so that the onions are translucent and softened, about 8 minutes. It's fine if the garlic starts to burn. Add the tomatoes and ¼ of the basil and bring the heat down to medium. Cook everything for 10 minutes more.

BLEND: Add the contents of the pot to the blender (you may have to do it in batches) and blend until completely smooth. When you are done, add everything back to the pot. Add the cream and season with salt and pepper.

Crank the heat up to medium high. The cream will start to thicken the soup and will turn it a light pink color. After about 5-7 minutes when the soup is thick, add the rest of the fresh basil.

Cook for another 2-3 minutes. Taste and re-season if necessary. Serve hot.

MAKES 4 SERVINGS

Cheddar Corn Chowder with Bacon

MATERIALS
1 large pot
Microwavable bowl
Wooden spoon
Cutting board
Chef's knife
Small plate lined with paper towels
Vegetable peeler

INGREDIENTS
1 16 oz package of frozen corn
2 tablespoons of butter
3 strips of bacon
2 medium sized potatoes (either regular or sweet potatoes), peeled and diced
1 medium onion, diced
2 carrots, peeled and diced
1 bay leaf
1 tablespoon rosemary
Salt and pepper
2 cups of cream or 1 12 oz can of coconut milk
¾ cup sharp cheddar cheese, or fontina, gruyere, white cheddar, etc.

My mother has some really funny demands. Sometimes it's just to vacuum or clean my room, and then other times it is sweet potato French fries or cheddar corn chowder. But more specifically than that, she asks for my grandma's corn chowder, which I don't know how to make.

My version of corn chowder is made with frozen corn instead of fresh corn and it has a lot of bacon and cream. It is seriously amazing! Try it one day when it's cold outside, but if you live in Miami, just crank down the air conditioning, put on a sweater and pretend you're in Oregon.

50 minutes

MICROWAVE: Place the frozen corn in the microwave with a couple tablespoons of water and cook for 3 minutes. Carefully drain the water and set aside.

PREP: Meanwhile, as the corn is defrosting, peel and slice the carrots and potatoes. It is important to chop the carrots into small pieces. If you have more experience with a knife, dice them into smaller cubes, but if not, don't worry about it. Dice the onion, and finely slice the bacon into pieces (about half an inch thick, but it doesn't have to be exact).

COOK: On high heat, add the bacon to the pot and allow it to crisp up. You should stir it frequently. After about 8 minutes, carefully remove the bacon from the pan and place the pieces on the plate lined with paper towels. Discard the excess oil, leaving about 2 tablespoons in the pan.

Still on high heat, add the corn, onions, carrots and potatoes to the pot, along with the white wine. Sauté them for about 2 minutes, just so that they can get some color. Fill the pot with water until all the vegetables are covered, and allow the vegetables to cook together and soften for 20 minutes. Season with salt, pepper, rosemary and the bay leaf, and cover.

When you return, the liquid should have reduced by more than half and the vegetable should be very soft. Add the 2 cups of cream, stir and taste.

Bring the soup down to a simmer on medium low heat, and allow it to cook for an additional 15-20 minutes. When you are done, the carrots should have all disappeared and the soup should be rich and thick. Add the cheese and stir until the cheese is incorporated throughout and melted. Taste and season if necessary. Remember to discard the bay leaf (because they are technically inedible) and serve the soup with the bacon bits on top.

MAKES 4 SERVINGS

Fried Calamari Salad

MATERIALS
Nonstick pan
Large bowl
Cutting board
Cooking tongs
Chef's knife
Plate lined with
paper towels
Small bowl
Whisk or spoon

INGREDIENTS
1 ½ pound calamari
(fresh or defrosted if
frozen)

1 cup flour
1 and 1/2 cups of cold
water, plus
additional 2
tablespoons
Salt and pepper
1 tablespoon basil
2 cups of vegetable
oil

Salad
2 heads of romaine,
or 1 large package of
lettuce greens (use
whatever you like,

and a variety if
available, see pg.)
2 carrots, peeled and
sliced thin
½ cup parmesan
cheese
2 large tomatoes,
diced

½ cup of
Steakhouse dressing
(see pg. 246)

I've tried fried calamari salads at a couple different restaurants, and every time I eat it, it's always completely different. My two favorites recipes come from two restaurants in Miami: The first one specializes in Caribbean food (Ortanique) and serves the salad with sweet and spicy carrots and a sweet tropical dressing, while the other place serves it extra crispy with a sweet and acidic red wine vinaigrette (China Grill). For this recipe I tried to combine my two favorite parts from each of the restaurants.

30 minutes

PREP: Slice the carrots lengthwise into long strips. They don't have to be very skinny, but don't make them to large either. Place them in the small bowl and add 1 cup of water. Place it in the microwave and cook for 2 minutes. We are trying to soften the carrots for the salad.

In the same package that you purchase them, simply run tap water over the calamari to take away any residual salt. *They shouldn't smell fishy: fresh seafood, no matter what it is, will smell slightly salty, like the sea.* Dry them and set them aside until you are ready to start frying.

When the carrots are done cooking, pick one up and feel it for doneness. They should still be crunchy, but slightly tender as well. Carefully remove them from the microwave and drain them of all the water. Place the bowl in the fridge until you are ready to use it so you don't get distracted by its presence!

TEMPURA: Make your tempura batter. Rinse off the bowl you used for the carrots and gradually add the cold water to the cup of flour, just until the batter is about the same thickness as a cake batter. Season with salt, pepper and basil.

FRY: Heat up the nonstick pan with the vegetable oil on high heat. Check the oil for readiness with a drop of the tempura batter: if the piece sizzles and doesn't sink to the bottom, then it is ready to fry. If it starts to splatter lower the heat, but not too much as the heat will naturally decrease as you add the calamari.

Coat the calamari completely and add them, one at a time, to the oil. *Remember try not to crowd the pan, as the cooking temperature will drop, resulting in a longer cooking time and running the risk of having really greasy calamari.*

Cook the calamari for about 3-4 minutes. All you are really trying to do is have a crispy batter on the outside. Calamari cook very quickly so once the batter on the outside is done, you'll know the insides are cooked to. Remove them from the pan and continue adding the remaining calamari. Drain the calamari on the paper towel lined plate and keep warm in an oven set at 200 degrees until you are ready to serve.

ASSEMBLE: Add the lettuce and tomatoes to the large bowl and toss the leaves so that everything is covered with dressing (see the next page for instruction). You don't want the dressing to be too heavy though but just enough to coat the leaves.

When you are ready to serve, add the calamari. Sprinkle with carrots and enjoy.

MAKES 6-8 SERVINGS

TRY: See pg. 48 for some ideas on what types of lettuce to use.

Steakhouse Dressing

MATERIALS
1 jar
1 knife
1 spoon

INGREDIENTS
1 1/3 cups olive oil
1/3 cups lemon juice
3 tablespoons honey

2 tablespoons red wine (or balsamic) vinegar
2 tablespoons Dijon mustard
Salt and pepper

I made this dressing originally for the spicy calamari salad, but it can be used for any occasion. This dressing combines the some of the sweetness from the lemon vinaigrette, with a subtle spice from the vinegar and mustard. Go all out and pair this salad with some frisee, arugula, or other lettuces for a modern take on a boring side dish.

5 minutes

SHAKE: Combine the lemon juice, honey, vinegar and mustard. Season with salt and pepper. Pour in the olive oil, close the jar and shake it up.

After about 20 seconds of shaking, it should have the texture of a dressing. Taste the dressing with a piece of lettuce, season if necessary and set aside until you are ready to serve. Shake up the dressing just as you are ready to serve, and toss it into the salad at the last minute so the lettuce doesn't wilt.

MAKES 1 ¼ CUPS OF DRESSING

Stuffed Potatoes

MATERIALS
2 microwavable bowls
Baking sheet
Spoon
Cutting board
Chef's knife
Plate lined with paper towels

INGREDIENTS
2 large potatoes
2 tablespoons of butter
2 strips bacon
2 tablespoons of sour cream
2 tablespoons of olive oil
Parmesan cheese to garnish

When I was in elementary school, we had disgusting food, but if you learned to sweet talk the lunch ladies like I did, they would sometimes sneak you the lunch reserved for teachers, which frequently were baked potatoes.

These potatoes combine the texture of mashed potatoes with baked potatoes. Stuff them with anything you want, and you can use the leftovers to make potato skins.

20 minutes

Preheat the oven to 400 degrees.

PREP: Place the strips of bacon on the plate and microwave for 2 minutes, until the bacon is brown and crispy. Meanwhile, slice the potatoes in half lengthwise and place them in the microwave as well. Cook for 7 minutes, or until they are fork tender. As the potatoes are cooking, chop the bacon into smaller pieces. When the potatoes are finished, scoop out the potato from the interior and place into the large bowl but be careful not to scoop all of it out. Leave about a ½ inch border of potato all around, so that you have a bed to put the filling back onto while you are baking it (and so the filling won't spill out when you cook them).

BAKE: Add the emptied out potato skins to the baking sheet and add 1 tablespoon of olive oil to prevent anything from sticking. Bake the skins as you are making the filling, which should only take 3 minutes. They really won't look very different than when you put them in, but by baking them, it will help form a nice bed for our filling.

As the potatoes shells are baking, season the filling that we just scooped out with salt and pepper. Add the sour cream, butter and bacon and mix until everything is smooth. Taste and season again if necessary.

BROIL: Add the filling back to the potato shells so that they are stuffed (see picture for reference).

Top the potatoes with parmesan cheese and a little bit more olive oil to help them brown. Broil on high for about 5 minutes. When the potatoes are finished, they should have a nice golden brown crust on top. Allow them to cool for a couple minutes and serve.

MAKES 4 SERVINGS

Risotto

MATERIALS
Pot
Nonstick pan
Wooden spoon
Ladle (or measuring cup)

INGREDIENTS
2 cups of Arborio rice (the package may also say risotto rice), but if you can't find that, short grain sushi rice works just as well
6 cups of chicken stock (low sodium) with an extra 1 cup of water, if needed
3 cloves of garlic, chopped finely
3 tablespoons of olive oil
4 tablespoons of butter
1/2 cup of milk
3/4 cup of grated parmesan cheese
3/4 cup of wine **
Salt and pepper to taste

Risotto is a great dish because it can serve a lot of people at once, and this recipe is amazing! When I made it for my friends, I fed ten people for less than 10 dollars, and I still had half a container of rice left. The only downside to making risotto is that it requires constant stirring, and should be served as soon as it is done.

When making risotto, don't portion it in terms of rice because it expands a lot when it cooks. For example, 3 cups of risotto can feed 10 people. Risotto is made better with wine, so if you have access to it, by all means, use it!

30 minutes

ASSEMBLE: Add all the stock into the large pot and bring up the heat to medium. Add fresh vegetables and herbs if you want to flavor it but you don't have to.

BEGIN: Heat up the olive oil in a pan on medium high heat and add the garlic and rice. Sauté together for about 2 minutes. When the garlic starts to darken in color (you'll also be able to smell it), begin adding the liquid.

Add the liquid one cup at a time (use the ladle or measuring cup)- if you add it faster, it won't come out the same way. The thing about risotto is that you have to keep stirring constantly (don't go crazy, just about one stir every 3 seconds). Once the liquid has reduced, add the next cup of stock, and repeat until you have used up all the liquid, about 25 minutes.

When the last of the liquid is just evaporating, I run a fork through the rice to test for doneness. There should be very little resistance throughout. Take a taste of it, and it should be tender but not falling apart. The same way Italians regard their pasta as al-dente, is the way you should regard the rice. If the rice is still too firm, add an additional cup of water or stock and cook until the liquid is evaporated. The rice should be soft, but still slightly firm and definitely not falling apart or clumping together.

Before all the liquid has finally evaporated is when you should add the wine, butter and milk. Just throw it all in. The butter and milk will thicken the risotto as well. To finish, add the parmesan cheese and flat leaf parsley. Season to taste with salt and pepper (I do this at the last minute because the cheese is salty) and serve

IMMEDIATELY.

YIELDS 6- 8 SERVINGS One cup of uncooked rice will feed 3-4 people.

IMPRESS: Add ingredients that you like, but try to find things that are in season. Diced tomatoes are great in the summer and make the risotto slightly pink in color.

DON'T add more than 2 or 3 ingredients.

TRY: Add shrimp (if you like them). Just add them at the same time you would add the butter, milk and cheese and just stir them in until they are completely cooked.

NOTE: The ratio of chicken stock is about 1 cup of rice to 3 cups of stock. I like to put in vegetables like carrots and onions, and fresh herbs like rosemary, to infuse into the stock. *Chicken bouillon cubes also works well* (simply follow the directions on the package). Don't forget to use wine.

Burano, Italy (above), home to some of the best risotto I've ever had. The island is off the coast of Venice and is accessible only by boat, but if you have a chance, visit Da Romano (below).

Braised Short Ribs

MATERIALS
1 nonstick pan with lid
1 plate
A fork
Kitchen tongs

INGREDIENTS
3 ½ pounds of short ribs
2 tablespoon each of rosemary and thyme
3 tablespoons each of salt and pepper
4 tablespoons each of butter and olive oil
3 cloves of garlic, peeled
2 large onions, sliced
2 large carrots, peeled and diced into bite size pieces
2 cups red wine
1 bay leaf
2 1/2 cups of cranberry juice cocktail
6 cups of beef stock

An interesting story I have about braised short ribs took place in New York City while I was eating at one of my dream restaurants, Jean Georges, with one of my friends, Cat.

Jean Georges is a 3 star Michelin restaurant (for the food world, think of that as winning Movie of the Year at the Oscars). It is formal and its menu is full of unfamiliar French food cooking preparations. When I suggested to Cat that she should try the short ribs because they sounded great, I was taken aback when she said a definitive no. I asked her why and at first she said it was because she didn't like ribs.

As it later turned out, she thought the short ribs were like regular ribs and she didn't want to be seen picking it up and gnawing on it in such a nice restaurant. So I explained to her what short ribs were and she agreed to order them. Without a doubt, it was probably one of the best things we've ever eaten.

Short ribs are smaller, meatier versions of regular beef and are usually braised for a long time to make them tender. They have one bone, but you eat them more like steak than ribs. Use your oven instead of the stove and you can cut the time in half. Because they cook down a lot, you may need to buy more than you think. This meat can also be a little expensive (about 4-5 dollars a pound), so reserve this dish for special occasions, or buy it when it is on sale.

2 hours and 15 minutes

MARINATE: An optional, but recommended step, especially if you are planning on eating these later in the week. Place the short ribs in a bowl and cover it with salt, pepper and rosemary. Add about a cup of red wine, a couple tablespoons of olive oil. Let it sit in the fridge for a couple of hours, or up to 2 days.

Preheat the oven to 350 degrees.

PREP: Smash the garlic with the side of the knife to remove the skin and thinly slice the onions. Peel the carrots and chop it into large, bite size pieces (just split each carrot into 3).

BROWN: Heat up the nonstick pan on high heat with 2 tablespoons of olive oil and 1 tablespoon of butter. Add ½ of the meat. *Remember you don't want to crowd the pan, because it will drop the cooking temperature.* All we're doing is browning.

If you marinated the meat, remove the meat from the marinade and add as it is. DO NOT discard the marinade because it will help form the sauce later.

If you are simply beginning the recipe right now, season the meat with salt, pepper. It's important to not be stingy and make sure that every side of meat is covered.

Brown the meat for about 2 minutes on each side. *Don't toss the meat around the pan because it won't be able to brown as well.* Simply add them to the pan and leave them there for 2 minutes, and then turn them over.

When all the pieces of meat are browned, place them on the plate and continue browning the remaining short ribs. Add the last 2 tablespoon of oil just to prevent the meat from sticking.

ASSEMBLE: Discard all but 2 tablespoons of oil into the so that the stew isn't greasy. On medium high heat, add the onions and season with salt and pepper. Brown the onions for about 5 minutes, but it isn't important to cook everything all the way through since they're going to be stewing.

Use the onions to form a base for the stew. Add the short ribs back to the pan, along with about 2 cups of red wine. Add the cranberry juice, carrots, beef stock, garlic, and bay leaf. Bring everything to a boil.

When the whole stew in boiling, cover the stew and place it in the oven. Cook at 350 degrees for 2 hours, but check on it after 1 hour and 45 minutes.

When it is finished, the stew should be much thicker and the meat should be fork tender. Use a fork to test the meat. You should be able to pull it right from the bone.

FINISH: As is, the stew would be great to serve, but I like to finish the stew a little further. **Remember the pan will be hot**, so carefully remove it from the oven and take out the meat and the carrots.

There will be a layer of fat above the stew because the fat would have rendered down. Use a spoon and try to skim off the top layer. It won't be possible to remove everything unless you freeze it so do the best you can, but don't sweat it if you can't.

Remove the meat and carrots from the pan and place it on a plate, so we can finish the sauce, which is done by adding back the excess marinade that we kept and an additional ½ cup of cranberry juice. Bring everything to a boil and allow it to boil for an additional 10 minutes so that the liquid reduces considerably into a thick, almost syrup like consistency.

Add a tablespoon of butter, place the carrots and the short ribs back into the stew, cover and keep warm until you are ready to serve.

MAKES 6-8 SERVINGS

Roasted Salmon with Panko and Pesto

MATERIALS
Baking sheet or roasting pan
Blender
Spoon
Spatula
Chef's knife
Aluminum foil

INGREDIENTS
One 2 pound salmon filet (the size is really unimportant because this recipe can be made for large groups as well as small dinners, and the leftover pesto can be stored)
Salt and pepper
1 cup pesto recipe (see pg. 266)
1 cup panko breadcrumbs
2 tablespoons of olive oil

I have to be honest here: I hate salmon. Hate it! And my family loves it, especially my mom, who I think heard Oprah say it was good for the skin or something, so thank you Oprah!

We recently had a family dinner and I volunteered to make the salmon just so it wouldn't look bad when I didn't eat it. Lo and behold, my dad comes in with a freaking mammoth of an animal lying in a cooler, and I had to filet and debone the beast with a samurai sword. When I finally cooked it and served it to everyone, they loved it, so I included it here for all the salmon lovers.

Salmon, by nature, is a very oily fish, so it can stand up to a lot of flavors. Don't be afraid to put whatever you want on it. You can substitute other fish for this recipe as well, but salmon is the most widely available.

40 minutes

Preheat the oven to 400 degrees.

PREP: Make the pesto (pg. 266) or buy it if you don't have enough time.

Line the baking sheet (or roasting pan) with aluminum foil. Place the fish on top of the foil.

Apply the pesto to the fish with a spoon. You want a nice, thick layer so be pretty liberal with the sauce. Pour it towards the center of the fish and gradually spread it out with the back of a spoon. It's okay if it falls off the fish; just make sure everything is nice and coated.

At this point, you can let the fish sit for a while, but if you're hungry now start applying the panko breadcrumbs, which will form a crunchy crust: using your fingers, pour the panko on top of the entire fish, making sure to get every corner coated with a thin crust. Drizzle some olive oil onto of the panko, which will help the fish brown.

BAKE: Bake or roast for 25 minutes. Check the salmon at 20 minutes, because it will cook differently depending on its shape and thickness. The outside crust should be a golden brown color and should be able to see a little bit of the pesto through it. The salmon should be pink and flaky on the inside.

Allow the salmon to rest for about 5-10 minutes. Cover it with another piece of aluminum foil to keep it warm until you are ready to serve. This recipe goes great with simple couscous or a really simply pasta as well.

MAKES 6-8 SERVINGS

Chicken Marsala

MATERIALS
Nonstick pan
Cutting board
Chef's knife
Wooden spoon
Kitchen tongs
Plastic bag
Plate

INGREDIENTS
2 boneless skinless chicken breasts
½ cup flour
Salt and pepper
1 cup of red wine
2 tablespoons butter
½ cup chicken stock
3 tablespoons of olive oil
2 tablespoons of cream (optional)
1 teaspoon rosemary or thyme

Chicken marsala, chicken Madeira and chicken with a red wine reduction are all about the same thing. All the pieces of chicken are cooked the same way, and the only difference is the type of wine the chicken is finished with. There are a hundred of different variations you can make with chicken and wine, so here is the basic technique.

20 minutes

PREP: Slice the chicken breasts in half lengthwise, so you are left with two identical and thinner pieces of chicken. Season both sides of the chicken with rosemary (or thyme), salt and pepper.

Throw the flour into the plastic bag and add the chicken. Shake it around until the chicken is completely coated.

COOK: Add the olive oil to the pan and bring the heat up to medium high. Allow the pan to heat up for about 1-2 minutes; then add the chicken. The chicken should gently sizzle. *If you start hearing a popping noise and the oil starts flying at you, lower the heat to medium and step away.* Don't be afraid though because the chicken will cause the heat in the pan to rapidly decrease. Remember not to cram all the chicken into your pan, so you might have to do it in batches. *If your pan isn't big enough, too much chicken will cause the heat to drop down too much and the chicken won't cook, or if they're overlapping, they'll just steam instead of pan fry.* Do it in batches if necessary.

Cook the chicken for 4-5 minutes per side. Allow it to sit in the pan- you don't need to keep moving it around. Flip the chicken over and it should be a nice golden brown color. Continue cooking the chicken for an additional 3-4 minutes. When both sides are golden brown, remove it from the pan and place it on the plate. Keep it warm in the oven at 170 degrees while we make the sauce.

SAUCE: The sauce couldn't be simpler. The best way to do this is by using the wooden spoon. On medium high heat again, add one tablespoon of butter to the pan and add the chicken stock. Deglaze the pan by scraping the pieces of chicken that might have gotten stuck to the bottom.

After about 30 seconds of scraping, add the red wine and bring the heat up to high. You need to get things boiling to cook out the liquid. (Optional) Add the cream, stir, and allow the sauce to continue cooking on high. The cream will lighten the color of the sauce quite a bit. Allow the sauce to reduce for 5 minutes.

You'll notice that the sauce will be thick and the liquid should have reduced in volume by half. Add the last tablespoon of butter and turn off the heat. Stir in the butter and wait for it to melt. Add the chicken back to the pan and coat it with sauce, which will also help warm up the chicken again. Serve.

MAKES 2 SERVINGS

Herb Marinated Lamb

MATERIALS
Non stick pan
Kitchen tongs
Freezer bag
Paper towels
Aluminum foil

INGREDIENTS
1 pound of lamb shoulder
3 cloves of garlic, smashed and left whole
1/2 cup balsamic vinegar
1/4 cup soy sauce (optional, but don't go out and buy it if you don't have it)
2 tablespoons rosemary
1 tablespoon salt
2 tablespoons pepper
2 tablespoons olive oil
2 tablespoons butter
1/2 cup red wine (optional but recommended)

For a lot of people, lamb can be a touchy subject. In the Philippines, where my mother is from, it isn't typically eaten at all. And then you have people like France's Charles de Gaulle (the General) who served it for family dinners almost every Sunday.

Lamb has a very distinct taste and some cuts of it can also be very expensive. I like to use lamb shoulder because it is tender and inexpensive, but it also because it has a very muted taste and cooks very quickly. The trick to lamb is to marinate it beforehand. Serve it with **mint jelly** and couscous and you're twenty minutes from amazing.

20 minutes

PREP: Do this as soon as you get home from the store so you're all you need to do is cook it when you get hungry. Place the lamb, garlic, balsamic vinegar, soy sauce and rosemary in the freezer bag. Season with salt and pepper. Shake it up a little bit. Let it sit for at least 1/2 hour, or overnight if you can.

PAN SEAR: Remove the lamb from the marinade and dab it a little bit with the paper towels. We are trying to remove the moisture because then lamb will brown better that way. Do NOT discard the marinade, as we will turn that into a sauce after.

Heat up the pan on high and add the olive oil. When the

pan is hot (wait about two minutes) add the lamb and a dab of butter. Immediately bring down the heat to medium high. *The lamb should immediately start to sizzle, but the oil shouldn't fly all over the kitchen.*

Allow it to sear (meaning don't touch it in the pan) for about 5 minutes. Lower the heat to medium, and flip. It should have a nice dark brown color. Continue to cook for an additional 5-7 minutes for medium. *If you don't like eating meat medium, then this really isn't the dish for you, because if you cook it too long, it will become like jerky.*

The best way to tell when meat is done is through touch. When you poke the meat, it should be firm and the meat should spring back in its place. If it feels like the center of your palm, it still needs to cook.

When the lamb is done, remove it from the pan and cover it with aluminum foil. Like any meat, it's important to let it cool before slicing into it, otherwise the juice will run all over the place, and you'll be left with a

hardcover book. Let it sit for about 10 minutes.

SAUCE: While the meat is resting, you can make the sauce. Sometimes the lamb lets off a lot of oil, so discard some of the excess oil left in the pan. Make sure you don't discard the bits that have settled on the bottom of the pan, as those will help flavor the sauce.

On medium heat, throw the marinade into the pan. Add the red wine and bring everything to a boil. Allow the sauce to reduce in volume by half (it should take about 5-7 minutes). You can add 2 tablespoons of cream at this point if you like. Taste and season.

Finish the sauce with the last tablespoon of butter. I always like finishing sauces with butter. Turn off the heat and just let the butter melt.

Serve the meat, and with a spoon, ladle over some of the sauce so that it looks straight out of a restaurant.. Serve with couscous, potatoes, rice or whatever you want.

MAKES 3 SERVINGS

Below: Herb Marinated Lamb. For best results, serve with roasted potatoes and mint jelly. Right: Risotto.

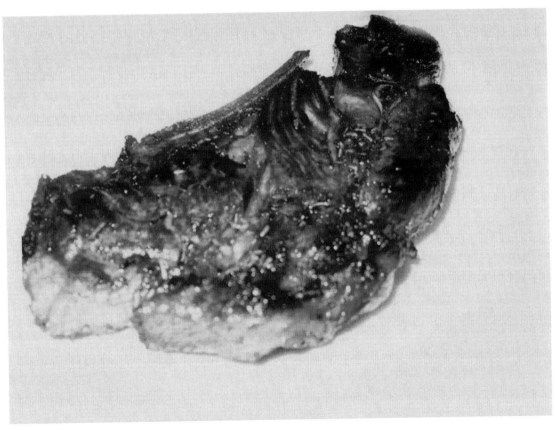

Roast Pork Chops with Apples

INGREDIENTS
Nonstick pan
Kitchen tongs
Cutting board
Chef's knife
Vegetable peeler
Meat thermometer (optional)
Wooden spoon

MATERIALS
2 large pork chops, about 1 inch thick
2 tablespoons olive oil
2 tablespoons brown sugar
1 tablespoon salt
1 tablespoon pepper
1 tablespoon thyme

2 golden delicious apples, peeled and roughly chopped into 2 bite pieces (or whatever apple you have)
1 cup apple juice
1 tablespoons butter
1 tablespoon flour
1/3 cup of water

I really love great pork chops but sometimes when you go to the grocery store, they only have the little stupid baby pork chops that dry up when you cook them.

When you buy pork chops, try and buy the thicker cuts; they may be a little more expensive, but you'll thank me later.

This might be an American thing, but my dad and grandmother love to eat pork chops with apple sauce, and the best way to serve this is with a sweet apple sauce made from the pan drippings.

30 minutes

Preheat the oven to 400 degrees.

PREP: Peel the apples with the vegetable peeler. Stand them up and slice them in half, splitting the apple down the core. Turn the halves onto their flat sides and split them in half again. Now you quartered the apple.

To remove the seeds, make a diagonal cut into the core of the apple. The core should fall out in one motion. Continue to core the rest of the quarters and then roughly chop the apples into bite size pieces.

BROWN: Heat the nonstick pan on high heat and add the oil. Season the meat with the brown sugar, thyme, salt and pepper just so that every piece of the meat is covered. Place the chops into the pan and cook for 3-4 minutes, until they are completely browned. Flip them over and add the apples.

Immediately, place the pan into the oven to roast.

ROAST: Roast the pork for about 12-15 minutes, or until the pork has reached an internal temperature of 160 degrees. *The apples should be a nice dark brown color as well, and should be fork tender.*

You can use a meat thermometer if you are unsure, but I just press my fingers again the meat. *It should be really firm, and the meat should spring back when you touch it.* Remove it from the oven and place it on the cutting board to rest for about 5-10 minutes. Cover it with foil to keep it warm. Remove the apples and set aside.

SAUCE: Making the sauce is easy and you can make it while the meat rests.

Drain the oil from the pan, leaving about 2 tablespoons in the pan, along with the apples. Bring the heat up to medium high heat and add flour to the pan. You are making a roux, which will thicken your sauce. When the flour has all dissolved into the liquid, it should be a light tan color, and it should be about the texture of a thin batter. If it begins to clump up too much, don't worry because the juice will thin it out.

Add the apple juice and the water, and continue to stir. As you are stirring, try and pick up any of the bits that may have settled on the bottom of the pan. You should see the sauce beginning to come together. Continue to stir and allow it simmer for 5 minutes, just so that the flavors can come together. When the sauce is thick, spoon it over the pork chops, along with the roasted apples and serve.

MAKES 2 SERVINGS

Steamed Mussels

MATERIALS
1 pot, with lid
Wooden spoon
Cutting board
Chef's knife
Large bowl
Strainer
Aluminum foil

INGREDIENTS
2 pounds of fresh mussels
½ cup flour
4 cloves garlic, chopped
2 tablespoons olive oil
½ cup dry white wine (buy a large bottle, and serve the rest with dinner)
1 very ripe small tomato, chopped
Salt and pepper
1/2 cup cream
2 tablespoons dried basil

Mussels, or *moules* in French, can be expensive, which is why I was hesitant to include this recipe in the first place, but if it wasn't for the somewhat steep price, this meal would be the perfect gourmet college dinner (its vegetarian, its healthy, can be eaten with your hands and it can be made in one pot very quickly). A mussel is cooked the minute it opens up, so a whole pot can be made in less than 10 minutes. Serve these with a French baguette, French fries and a green salad in traditional bistro style.

BTW: Do not buy mussels at the grocery store that are open. That means they are dead and not fresh.

10 minutes

PREP: In the large bowl, pour in the mussels. Fill it with cold water and add the flour. Add some ice if you have it to the bowl (about two handfuls) and allow the mussels to sit for ten minutes. *All we're really trying to do is remove the sand and dirt and for some reason, the flour helps remove the sand.* When you are ready to cook, rinse out the mussels and dry them thoroughly with a kitchen towel.

CUT: Smash the garlic with the side of your knife and mince. Chop the tomatoes and the parsley.

COOK: On high heat, add the olive oil, garlic and tomatoes to the pot and cook everything for about 1 minute.

Add the white wine and mussels, cream and basil and season everything with salt and pepper. *You don't need to use that much salt because the mussels themselves are pretty salty to begin with.*

Cover the mussels and allow them to cook between 8-10 minutes. Shake them in the pot every minute or so just to make sure they are moving around. DO NOT TAKE OFF THE LID. The steam is what cooks them, and we need to maintain a constant cooking environment.

Check on the mussels at 8 minutes. If they are open already, they are done. Turn off the heat and serve.

If they are just beginning to open, allow them to cook for 1 ½ more minutes still covered, then turn off the stove remove them from the heat. If they are halfway open at 8 minutes, then turn off the heat and allow them to sit where they are for 1 ½ minutes. Mussels cook quickly and they will to continue to cook once they are out of the pan. Serve in bowls with crusty bread to dip into the sauce.

MAKES 4 SERVINGS

IMPRESS: If you are making this at home (and not at school), get your parents to buy you *saffron* for the sauce. It is the most expensive spice in the world and made from crocus flowers, but it is classic for this recipe. All you need is a very small pinch though, less than half a teaspoon.

Skirt Steak

INGREDIENTS
1 baking sheet
Kitchen Tongs
Cutting board
Chef's knife
Aluminum foil

MATERIALS
One 2 pound skirt steak
4 tablespoons of salt (2 per side)
4 tablespoons of pepper (2 per side)

Chimichurri Sauce
1/2 cup olive oil
3 cloves of garlic
¾ cup of fresh parsley
Salt and pepper
1 lemon, juiced
¼ cup red wine or balsamic vinegar (recommended, but don't go out and buy it if you don't have it; just buy an extra lemon)

Skirt steak goes by a lot of names, but if you've ever been to a Brazilian or Argentinean steak house, or churrascaria, that have become more and more frequent around the US, then you already know the Spanish word for it: churrasco. Traditionally, churrasco is seasoned only with salt to show off the quality of the meat, and it is often served alongside a chimichurri sauce, which is a sauce made from parsley, garlic and olive oil.

PS: Remember this next time you go to one of those all- you- can- eat steak houses: they make the meat salty on purpose. It makes you thirsty, and the water fills up your stomach. So resist the urge to keep drinking, and you'll leave with your money's worth.

20 minutes

PREP: It's important that the skirt steak is relatively the same width throughout to ensure an even cooking time. If you feel comfortable doing it yourself, slice the steak lengthwise- try to keep it under an inch in width. If you don't feel comfortable, ask the guy at the meat counter to do it for you.

BROIL: Preheat the oven to broil. Position the rack on the highest notch of your oven so that it can really get some color, but make sure the steak isn't touching the broiler. There should be about a good 4 inches between the steak and broiler. *A way to make sure you don't forget the meat when you are broiling is to leave the oven door slightly ajar.* Then you can see how the meat is cooking.

It's really going to depend on how thick your steak is for the length of time it will cook. The steaks I use are about ¾-1 inch thick, and I allow the broiler to get hot for about 5 minutes.

Place the steak into the oven and cook for 3 minutes.

Remove the steak from the oven and flip. Allow the steak to cook for another 3 minutes. At the 6 minute mark, pull out the steak.

Remember to keep an eye on the steak. Touch the meat. If you are met with resistance and the meat pushes back when you touch it, then you are at about medium heat. *Clench your non dominant hand into a fist, and a medium steak will feel like the skin at the point between your thumb and index finger.*

If you feel more comfortable, insert a meat thermometer into the steak. Steak doneness is taken in intervals of about 5 degrees. 140- 150 degrees is medium, over 165 is well done, and under 140 is approaching rare.

Let it rest of 10 minutes, covered in foil.

MAKES 4-6 SERVINGS

SAUCE: As the meat is cooking, add all the ingredients into a blender and blend for 1 minute.

NOTE: Steaks will continue to cook as you let them rest.

BUYING SEAFOOD

Fish is very easy to buy, but sadly there is a real lack of great quality seafood south of New England and east of San Francisco. In Miami, our seafood quality sucks, which makes perfect sense since we're a peninsula. It isn't nearly as fresh as you would expect it to be and there are many indications as to how to recognize the freshness of fish.

Fish is seasonal and can be somewhat expensive, so check what's good and what's on sale. Ask the guy behind the counter what's fresh because he'll probably tell you the truth to preserve your business. *Also remember that it is the law for people who sell seafood to tell you where and how the seafood was obtained, so if you have any questions, by law, they should know the answer.*

I didn't want to incorporate too many seafood recipes into this book because it can be both expensive and hard to find on a consistent basis. But there are many great techniques in this book that can be applied to fish if you find what you're looking for.

IF THE FISH IS WHOLE:

Buying fish is like checking out a person: You look at the eyes, the body and are attracted by the smell.

SMELL. Fresh fish is very easy to identify if it is whole. Many grocery stores are very clever, and so there is a glass container blocking you from the fish, both to protect from contamination, but also to prevent you from smelling it. Fresh fish doesn't smell like fish. It smells like the sea, somewhat briny and salty. Always ask to smell it before you buy it, and ask them point blank when the fish came in.

TOUCH. The flesh of the fish should be firm, and should spring back a little when you touch it. Frozen fish that has been defrosted will contain a lot of moisture that when melted, will cause the interior of the fish to soak up some of the water. As a result, it will be pretty soft and spongy.

OBSERVE. The eyes should be clear and the color of the skin should be vibrant. I remember watching a show on how blue fin tuna are purchased in the *Tsukiji* market in Japan. A piece of the tail is cut off and the buyers move the flesh between their fingers I'm not sure what they're looking for, but I'm guessing it's to check out the oil content and fattiness. PS: *Don't rub your hand between someone's tail if you're checking them out*. This technique only works on fish, and you will get hit.

Obviously, in the grocery store, you can only see the fish, but if it's good you'll know it.

IF THE FISH IS FILETED:

A fresh fish will have a very smooth, unilateral filet. There won't be any marks or cuts because the proprietor will try and preserve what he has in order to get the best price for it. But the largest indicator is the flesh. If it looks spongy or soft, or if parts of the filet look slightly softer than the other parts, chances are it is not that fresh, and they simply kept it in the freezer and defrosted it. The sponginess is due to water that has been dispelled during the defrosting process.

STORING FISH:

Fish can be stored in the freezer but TRY TO AVOID IT. The problem is maintaining the freshness and firmness of the flesh while you defrost it. Simply allow it come to room temperature slowly. Julia Childs said that it should take almost 3 days to defrost a fish because you would want it to defrost as slowly as possible. She would keep the fish covered in ice in the fridge until it was completely defrosted.

But we don't have three days, so run some lukewarm water over it, or defrost it overnight. Or, better even, just buy it the day you want to cook it. Fish doesn't need to marinade.

SEAFOOD

Buying seafood is very much like buying fish. You should know what you're doing and what you're looking for. For example, seafood is very seasonal so make sure what you want to buy is in season. There is also a lot of frozen seafood available, like scallops and shrimp, which are actually good substitutes for their fresh counterparts because a lot of times grocery stores will just defrost their bagged shrimp and sell them like that anyways.

It is very important to smell anything that you buy beforehand. There are a lot of grocery stores that will try and sell you old stuff (that will make your house smell like low tide) and will shove them in the bag and tape them up as fast as possible.

BUYING CLAMS AND MUSSELS

I was always told to not buy shellfish during the summer. The reason why is because of red tide, which can accumulate in the shellfish and make it very unpleasant to digest. Now, a lot of commercial farmers, who are responsible for a lot of the shellfish we eat, are screened to maintain the highest level of safety, so if you were to eat these during the summer, you'll be alright.

Clams and mussels are very easy to identify when they are great. If they are closed, they are alive and if they are open, they are dead. *Don't purchase open shellfish.* After you cook them, if there are some that don't open, simply discard them or you run the risk of getting sick.

SOAK: Place the clams and mussels in a large bowl of water with ½ cup of flour for every pound of mussels and stir it around. The flour will help remove the excess dirt from inside the shells. I also put ice in the water to keep it cold.

STORE: These are best eaten fresh. Do not store in the freezer. Keep in the fridge in a plastic bag on ice (as cold as possible without freezing them) until you are ready to serve them. The bag will prevent them from absorbing the water as it melts.

BUYING SCALLOPS

There are two main varieties of scallops: *sea scallops* (which are the larger ones) and *bay scallops*. These should also be avoided during the summer, unless you purchase frozen ones, which were probably harvested during peak season.

I once purchased old scallops and neglected to smell them, so when I got home and began cooking them, it was really an awful aroma. If this happens and you can't return them (seriously, if they are bad, return them, and if you are embarrassed to, contact me through email and I'll call them for you), place them in milk and allow them to soak for at least a half an hour.

STORE: Cold as well.

BUYING SHRIMP

Shrimp is probably the most accessible of all the shellfish, and there are a lot of varieties available from all over the world. Shrimp are measured in numbers. For example, if you see something that says 20 24, that means there's approximately 20 to 24 shrimp per pound. Also remember that if you buy fresh shrimp from the grocery store, see if you can get them peeled and deveined, otherwise you'll have to pull out the digestive tract by yourself and that's pretty messy work.

Shrimp is available both pre cooked or raw, and the raw shrimp will be grey in color. These are pretty much a safe bet, and are definitely some of the most affordable, if not most widely available, seafood option.

STORE: Shrimp can be stored cooked in the fridge or frozen. It's pretty resilient.

CALAMARI

I love calamari, but it took a while for me to start eating it. The first time I ever cooked it at home, I was trying to recreate the same salad featured in this book. When I went to the grocery store, I knew I was buying squid, but when I didn't see 'calamari', I opted to buy squid rings instead. It was a big mistake.

Calamari, as we know it, has a much more delicate taste than regular squid. When you are looking for calamari, there are going to be a lot of things that sound very similar, like 'squid rings', but don't fall for it like I did.

The best way to prep calamari is to let it soak for a little bit in water or milk to remove some of the salt. Allow it to sit for about 15 minutes.

STORE: I try to avoid storing calamari. Buy it the day you want to cook it.

ENTERTAINING

THE ART OF
Entertaining

I began making large, multicourse dinners for my friends when I was in high school. At first, I made every mistake imaginable, but slowly, I found some tricks that saved me both a lot of time and energy. Here are some ways to entertain on a college budget.

Drinks.

Buy two different types of sodas, like Coke or Sprite, which you know everyone likes. If someone doesn't like it, they can always have water. If you are planning on drinking, buy drinks that are also good mixers, but don't buy more than two mixers. If people ask what they should bring, tell them drinks because they're cheaper and will always be consumed. Get a pitcher of water too and set it out on the table so people can pour for themselves.

Appetizer.

When your friends arrive, they will be hungry, so by feeding them bread or some form of carbohydrate or starch at the beginning of the meal, not only will they end up eating more, they will also get full faster.

Use the grocery store if you have to. Buy a variety of cheese (chevre, gruyere, Manchego, brie) or ham (prosciutto, Serrano, salami), and serve with crackers or French baguette. You can also buy some potato chips, toasted nuts or chips with salsa. If you're really cool, try something unexpected, like edamame.

First Course.

Screw the salad. I've made salad on several different occasions and believe me, people are not impressed by it, not matter how good it is. Just forget about it. Unless you are EXTREMELY confident in the kitchen, your first course should NEVER be something fried because you run the risk of making a mess in front of your friends. It should be something bite size that doesn't require plates or utensils. A good example is the spinach and artichoke dip. Simply cook it before and keep it warm in the oven until you are ready to serve.

Main Course.

Proteins like meat or fish should be the cornerstone of your meal, and I recommend only buying one type. Because it is the most expensive, it should be rationed to about 4-8 oz per person, depending on how many things you are serving. This trick benefits you, the chef, because not only do you have more time to focus on the ingredient, but you save money and you don't run the risk of having your friends compare the two main courses that you made, especially if they ended up liking the cheaper one.

Side dish.

The first rule of choosing a side dish is the law of balance: a heavy main course should be a lighter side dish, and vice versa. Carbohydrates and starches are your friend. Large dinners should always have both an appetizer and a side dish that is either one of the two. Most of the time, people also expect a side dish of that nature, so it works out for everyone. Remember to mix it up.

Dessert.

Use your grocery store: people always have room for dessert, and there are a lot of great varieties and great options to choose from. Try to choose something familiar like brownies or cheesecake to avoid running the risk of someone developing an allergic reaction.

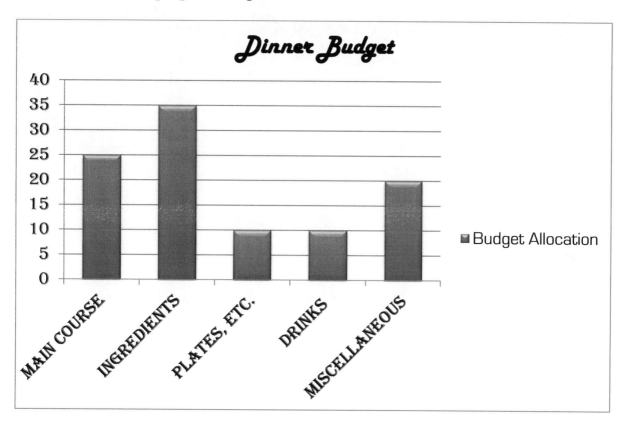

Main course (25%), Remaining Ingredients (35%), Plates, Napkins, etc. (10%), Non Alcoholic Drinks (10%), Miscellaneous (20%).

If you are making time sensitive food, tell everyone to arrive 30 minutes earlier than when you expect them to be there, but this also means that you need to be ready by then. This system works because by the time your guests arrive, you'll look completely at ease because you've prevented yourself from procrastinating.

What should I bring?

If you're ever invited to a dinner, always ask the host if you should bring anything and even if your host tells you not to bring anything, buy a dessert. If you're getting invited to your girlfriend or boyfriend's parents' house, bring flowers or wine. If you're going to a house party, bring a handle or a 6 pack. If the host is a girl, bring her something made of chocolate. If the host is a guy, bring him something alcoholic. Play to your strengths but NEVER SHOW UP EMPTY HANDED!

Music

Music should not overwhelm the party. Think of it as the wait-staff of a restaurant: it's there in the background to help you, not interfere with your conversation. Put something pleasant, mainstream and upbeat, and make it background music so you're loud friends aren't competing with music to talk.

Decorations

NO. It's more money and clean up afterwards. If you want a theme, tell people how to dress, otherwise go out to a club afterwards. And especially, don't use candles if you're friends are going to be drinking after dinner.

Cooking with Your Guests

Many television personalities encourage the host to get your friends involved in the cooking, but here's my advice: DON'T. If you are taking the time to make something nice, and you're friends are dressed nicely, you're going to be responsible for apologizing to your girlfriend for spilling tomato sauce on her $200 shoes. Plus, dorm kitchens are small for a reason.

Clean up

If you are hosting the party, don't be embarrassed to accept help from those who offer- just don't expect everyone to offer it. If you clean as you cook, you shouldn't have a problem.

Setting a Table

In case you have any doubts, here are instructions on how to properly set a table.

- TABLE CLOTH OR PLACEMAT: It's one or the other, never both. If you are sitting down to a formal dinner, use a table cloth, if it is casual, you really don't need anything.
- LEFT OF THE PLATE: Salad fork on the far left and then the regular fork, which you place over a simply folded napkin. For a simpler setting, omit the salad fork. As you are eating, remember to start from the outside and move inwards.
- CENTER: Plate.
- RIGHT OF THE PLATE: Knife (the blade facing towards the plate) and a tablespoon, which serves as your soup spoon. For informal dinners, use the tablespoon for dessert and coffee.
- ABOVE THE KNIFE AND SPOON: Water glass, which should always be on the top right of the table setting. If you are drinking wine, the wine glass should be placed on its right.

EXTRAS

For formal dinners, these are small details that won't go unnoticed.

- BREAD PLATE: Always on the left hand side of the forks. If you own a set of butter knives, please invite me over to your dorm room.
- DESSERT FORK AND COFFEE SPOON: Place the fork directly in front of the plate, and the spoon behind it. If you're fancy, turn the fork to face right and the spoon to face left.
- COFFEE: Set the coffee cups aside because you won't have any room on the table. If you're really trying to impress someone, set each cup on a saucer.

Menu For Her

Bruschetta on pita chips (pg. 190 and 196)

~

Shrimp scampi (pg. 109)

~

Hot chocolate cake with (pg. 206)
Peanut Butter Sauce

~

Mint Tea

~

Buy a dry white wine and French bread. Feeling lucky? Listen to John Mayer.

45 MINUTES BEFORE ARRIVAL

1. Preheat the oven.

2. FILL A POT WITH WATER AND PLACE ON STOVE. You want to make the pasta at the last minute, even as she is talking to you and eating the bruschetta because leftover pasta will get really tough if it's allowed to sit around for a while. You just want the water to be ready when it is time. Remember to fill the pot about ¾ of the way up.

3. MAKE THE BRUSCHETTA. Bruschetta benefits from sitting around for a while so make it and store it in the fridge until you are ready. OMIT THE GARLIC IF YOU CHOOSE.

4. FINISH PREPPING THE SHRIMP. You already have the cutting board out. Finish chopping the basil, tomatoes, juicing the lemons, etc.

5. WASH YOUR HANDS.

6. PREP THE HOT CHOCOLATE CAKE. Mix everything in the mugs and store them in the fridge until you are ready to eat them. They only take 3 minutes to cook anyways.

7. WIPE DOWN THE CUTTING BOARD. Because you've been using a lot of ingredients, I would advise getting a plate and simply placing all the items that you recently prepped onto the plate. It will help you stay organized and will give you an opportunity to use the board.

8. CUT THE PITA CHIPS. Slice them and place them on the baking sheet (that you sprayed with cooking spray). If this is too much work, buy pita chips.

9. START COOKING THE SCAMPI. Add all the ingredients for the scampi and follow the directions up until you add the shrimp. DO NOT ADD THE SHRIMP until the very last minute (after she has arrived). OMIT GARLIC IF YOU CHOOSE.

10. CLEAN UP. It's always important to clean up as you are going along with the cooking, because it will make everything easier in the end, and it will also make it look like you know what you're doing.

11. SET THE TABLE. Pull out everything that you need and set the table, like the plates, bowls, serving spoons. This will force you to keep a clean cooking environment. (I would say a nice bowl with a spoon for the bruschetta, with a small plate for the pita chips. You will also need a large bowl for the pasta, but you can use your kitchen tongs to serve it)
    a. Get out the colander so you have something to drain the pasta into.

12. GET READY! You should have about 20 minutes to get ready, but let's be realistic: she's probably not going to arrive on time anyways.

10 MINUTES BEFORE ARRIVAL

1. Place the seasoned pita chips in the oven. You should have the bruschetta out right at the time she is supposed to arrive.

2. BEGIN BOILING THE WATER.

3. ARRIVAL: Be ready. *Tell her she looks great.* The kitchen should be clean, the dishes should be done and stored away, and everything that you need to still cook should be left. Give her something to drink as she arrives, like a white wine or Jack Daniels. (Just kidding).

15 MINUTES AFTER ARRIVAL

1. Bring the heat up on the pot. Because it is already hot (or boiling), you may just need to add the pasta. Make sure there is enough water in the pot. It should be able ¾ of the way filled. If not, add hot tap water to the pot and wait until it boils. Don't forget to season the water.

5 MINUTES BEFORE SERVING

1. Bring the sauce of the shrimp up to high heat and add the shrimp to the pan. If the sauce looks too thin add about ¼ cup of the pasta water. The shrimp should turn pink in 5 minutes.

2. FINISH. Drain the pasta and add it to the shrimp. Top it with basil and serve it on the table with bread.

3. DESSERT AND TEA. Microwave the cake. You're done!

Menu for Her

Orange chicken
with white rice (pg. 82 and 116)

~

Sautéed String Beans (pg. 131)

~

Chocolate Dipped Strawberries (pg. 215)

~

Espresso (pg. 40)

BUY: BREADSTICKS FROM THE GROCERY STORE FOR AN APPETIZER

My high school Latin American History teacher, DQ, told me to never show up empty handed because then you look like a jerk. Depending on the setting, it's sort of true. Get flowers.

1 HOUR BEFORE.

1. RICE. You can make it in the microwave or on the stove or in the rice cooker. It should take about 20 minutes, so it's best to just get this out of the way. When you're about to serve, just warm it up for a minute.

2. PREP. Finish chopping all the vegetables before you do the chicken (you want to leave the chicken for last because of cross contamination purposes). When you have everything set aside and finished, do the chicken.

3. BREAD THE CHICKEN. Place the flour in the bag and bread the chicken. Shake it up and just place it in the fridge as it is, until you're ready to use it.

4. MICROWAVE BLANCH STRING BEANS. Don't forget to run cold water or ice through them so that they maintain their crunch and their color.

5. CHOCOLATE SAUCE. Assemble the ingredients you'll need for the chocolate sauce. Also take the time to make sure your strawberries are washed cleaned and fresh.

6. CLEAN UP. Everything should be spotless.

7. SET THE TABLE. Get everything that you'll need when you serve. Also pull all the plates that you plan on serving on. Get all the ingredients ready that you'll need for the orange chicken by the stove so you're ready.

8. GET READY! You should have at least 30 minutes to get ready.

10 MINUTES BEFORE

1. Make the string beans. Keep them in the pan so you can toss them around on high heat just until they're hot.

2. ARRIVAL. Give her something to drink. Tell her she looks great and you like her new dress and shoes. Offer her some of the breadsticks. Because there isn't an appetizer for this menu, start cooking about 10 minutes after she arrives.

3. ORANGE CHICKEN. Make the recipe for orange chicken as directed. If the rice needs to be heated up again, do it.

4. FLASH SAUTE STRING BEANS. Heat up the string beans. This should be the last thing you do before you are ready to heat. It will only take about 2 minutes since everything is cooked through.

5. EAT DINNER.

6. DESSERT. Melt the chocolate with the cream until you have a really great sauce. Serve it warm on the table (in the same pot that you cooked it in) next to strawberries and dip yourselves.

7. DISHES. Don't worry, there really aren't that many, so don't freak out. Clean them up as soon as you have a chance and just get them out of the way so you don't have to worry about them later.

Menu for Him

Bacon wrapped cherry tomatoes (pg. 179)

~

Barbecue Ribs (pg. 87)

~

Twice baked potato (pg. 257)

~

Nutella Pizza (pg. 210)

2 HOURS BEFORE

If you want a wedding proposal, or a great birthday gift, cook your guy this meal and it's a done deal. You will need two baking sheets for this recipe.

1. PREHEAT THE OVEN.

2. SEASON THE RIBS, COVER AND BAKE. Remember to season the ribs all over.

3. THROW POTATOES INTO THE MICROWAVE.

4. MAKE THE CHERRY TOMATOES WITH BACON. Wrap the slices of bacon around the tomatoes and secure them with toothpicks. When you are done, line the baking sheet aluminum foil and set them on the baking sheet. DON'T PLACE THEM IN THE OVEN YET.

5. TWICE BAKED POTATOES. Finish making the twice baked potatoes. Place them on the baking sheet when you're done. For this recipe, you don't need to place the potatoes back into the oven as you are making the filling because they will be baking for a longer time anyways. DON'T PLACE THEM IN THE OVEN YET.

6. CLEAN UP EVERYTHING. SET THE TABLE.

7. GET READY. **You have approximately 1 HOUR AND A HALF to get ready. GOOD LUCK!**

15 MINUTES BEFORE

1. Remove the ribs from the oven. Check them: they should be tender and falling off the bone. Keep them covered with aluminum foil and allow them to sit on the stove until you are ready for them. Increase the cooking temperature to 400 degrees and place both the potatoes and the cherry tomatoes with bacon in the oven.

2. Remove the tomatoes when they are crispy, about 12 minutes. Place them on the table at the time he is supposed to arrive. Turn off the heat in the oven and let the potatoes sit in there. (The residual heat will continue to brown the potatoes so we DON'T have to broil them)

3. ARRIVAL. Give him a kiss. Give him the food and get him a drink.

10 MINUTES AFTER ARRIVAL.

1. Place the ribs back into the oven to warm up just a little bit. They should still be hot though. Warm them up at 300 degrees for about 5 minutes (with the aluminum foil removed). You can add more barbeque sauce if you want.

15INUTES AFTER.

1. He's starving and the cherry tomatoes are gone. Remove the potatoes from the oven. Using your chef's knife, cut the ribs in half (you don't have to cut each individual rib out). If you have leftover barbeque sauce, pour a little onto each of them.

40 MINUTES AFTER.

1. All the food is gone. He has eaten everything and loved it, and you're so full you can't look or think of food right now. He's watching TV right now, and you have the choice of making the Nutella pizza or not. He's going to say it's ok, you don't have to make it, but he really wants to try it.

2. WAIT AN HOUR AND A HALF BEFORE MAKING THE PIZZA. Follow the directions. If you don't want to make the pizza, go get dessert instead.

3. DISHES. If the food turned out really well, he might even volunteer to help, but no guarantees.

Steakhouse Menu

Garlic Bread (pg. 194)

~

Caesar Salad (pg. 54)

~

Steak au Poivre (pg. 98)

~

Twice Baked Potatoes (pg. 257)

~

Fried Oreos (pg. 208)

If you are really crazy, creamed spinach is a real classic steakhouse item, but I didn't want to overwhelm you.

30 MINUTES OF PREP

1. SEASON STEAK: Season everything you need to make and keep it in the fridge until you are ready to use it.

2. SALAD AND DRESSING. Make them separately, and add the dressing at the very end, at the table, right before you are ready to serve.

3. POKE THE POTATOES: Begin making the potatoes. Because it is a fast recipe, make it ahead, and heat it up just before serving.

4. FINISH MAKING THE POTATOES: Keep them in the oven just until you are ready to serve, and the residual heat will keep them warm.

5. CLEAN UP AND SET THE TABLE: Get everything (all the serving platters or plates that you want to serve the food on) in place.

6. GET YOURSELF READY.

15 MINUTES BEFORE

1. Take the steak out of the fridge because steak browns best when it is at room temperature. Also make sure you have the pan that you are going to make the steak in (or the baking sheet if you are going to broil the steak).

2. ARRIVAL. Get your guests drinks.

3. BREAD. Heat up the bread in the oven at 300 degrees for about 8 minutes, until it is hot. As it is cooking, make the garlic butter sauce, and serve it separately as a dipping sauce.

15 MINUTES AFTER ARRIVAL

1. Begin cooking the steak. It should take about 10 minutes (depending on what cut of meat you used). ALLOW IT TO REST FOR 10 MINUTES BEFORE SERVING: keep it warm by covering it in aluminum foil.

2. EAT.

3. CLEAN UP. Your friends can help clear the table. Just use the dishwasher.

4. WAIT AN HOUR TO MAKE THE OREOS.

Appetizer Menu

Guacamole (pg. 184)
or
Bruschetta (pg. 190)

Served with baked pita chips (pg. 196)
~
Tia Les' Fire House Chicken Wings (pg. 183)
~
Salt with Garlic Oil (pg. 186)

50 MINUTES

This day menu is multipurpose: it was written to both serve large groups and with items that could be served room temperature and that were easily transportable. Everything here can be eaten with your hands and nothing has to be refrigerated. It's also pretty healthy.

1. PREHEAT THE OVEN TO 350 DEGREES.

2. WINGS: These will take the longest to make, but once you place them in the oven, you can start on everything else. You will be done with everything (clean up time included) by the time the wings are finished.

3. PITA CHIPS: Make the pita chips and place them in the oven with the wings. When they are done, put them in their serving container until you are ready to serve them.

5. BRUSCHETTA AND CHOP EVERYTHNG ELSE: Make the bruschetta and chop the ingredients for the guacamole. Get out the containers or serving platters that you plan on putting them in.

4. REMOVE PITA CHIPS.

5. GUACAMOLE: Finish mashing. Don't forget to add lemon juice to prevent it from browning. Place it in the container.

6. COOK SHRIMP. Pack in container as well.

7. REMOVE THE CHICKEN WINGS FROM OVEN AND PACK.

8. CLEAN UP.

9. SERVE. Place all the ingredients in containers so you can transfer them to wherever you are having your party.

DON'T USE DISHES. As for drinks, people are going to be drinking out of cans and bottles anyways.

Drinking Nights

Loaded Nachos (pg. 201)

~

Asian Pizza (pg. 197)

~

LOTS OF WATER

The point of this menu is to help your drunk friends sober up and put food into your friends who are in the process of getting drunk. The directions for this menu are pretty easy because the pizza can be made in the oven, and the nachos can be made in the microwave.

1. PREHEAT THE OVEN.

2. ASSEMBLE PIZZA: Defrost the vegetables in the microwave. Start frying the chicken or use leftover chicken, whatever you may have. BAKE.

3. NACHOS: You want to serve the nachos first and the pizza second. From a practical standpoint, the nachos take the least amount of input, but by giving your friends nachos (that they eat bite by bite) you can easily identify what their tipping point might be, or whether they can actually hold down food. Save the pizza for later for your friends who are just hungry.

4. CLEAN UP AND SERVE. Cut slices into the pizza, and serve on the same baking sheet that you cooked it in. Serve the nachos on a giant tray and place in the center of the room.

Big Birthday Menu

Salt and Pepper Shrimp (pg. 189)

~

Green Salad of tomatoes, walnuts and honey balsamic (pg. 56)

~

Pineapple Express Fried Rice with chicken (pg. 114)

~

Roasted Asparagus (pg. 140)

~

Nutella Pizza (pg. 210)

Although this recipe includes a lot of components, it's very easy to pull together. This whole menu can also serve a lot of people, and because rice is the main course, it is also very cost effective. For the fried rice, you can buy a rotisserie chicken from the store that would be great- just remember to remove the skin.

1 HOUR

1. PREHEAT THE OVEN TO 400 degrees.

2. COOK RICE. This will take about 20 minutes, so use the microwave and you don't have to worry about it until you are ready to cook. For fried rice, I recommend using a variety called *parboiled* (see pg. 216 for explanation).

3. SALAD DRESSING: Make the salad dressing first and keep it in the fridge until you are ready to serve it. At that point, you will probably need to shake it up again to get the same consistency that you had before.

4. PREP: Slice all the ingredients that you will need for these recipes. (That includes the tomatoes, walnuts, all the ingredients for the rice, and the pizza). Trim the asparagus as well. Don't forget to microwave blanch any of the ingredients that you need for the rice.

5. ROAST ASPARAGUS. Two minutes before the asparagus is done, take it out of the oven. Turn off the oven and remove the asparagus.

6. SALAD: Place the lettuce and tomatoes into the salad serving bowl and store in the fridge.

7. FRIED RICE: Because this recipe has chicken, we are going to chop the chicken into mini bite size pieces first. It's important to be finished with all your vegetable chopping before this point, otherwise we have to rewash the cutting board. If you are cooking the chicken- in the nonstick pan, sauté the chicken for about 8 minutes, or until the chicken is browned and completely cooked through. Season with salt and pepper and set aside on a plate for later.
   a. Follow the directions for the fried rice.

8. COOK SHRIMP.

9. CLEAN UP EVERYTHING. Make sure you have all the serving plates and spoons ready for later.

10. SET UP BUFFET STYLE. Use Chinese takeout containers and chop sticks if you're a cool guy, and since were eating fried rice, it makes sense. This also helps minimize dishes.

11. GET READY.

15 MINUTES BEFORE

1. Place the shrimp on the serving platter and set it on the table. Make sure you have the drinks ready. Place the salad onto the table, but don't add the dressing until the very end.

2. ARRIVAL. People will begin helping themselves with food, and you'll be talking and passing out drinks. Place the asparagus in the

oven, which will be warm at this point, so that they can be warm when we're ready to heat.

3. SERVE SHRIMP AND SALAD.

4. Wait until everyone has arrived before you finish the fried rice.

30 MINUTES AFTER ARRIVAL.

1. Heat up the rice and serve on the table. DON'T FORGET THE ASPARGAUS in the oven.

2. RICE. Set out the pot that you used to cook the rice in directly on the table, and people can just spoon the rice into their containers.

3. WAIT AN HOUR BEFORE MAKING THE PIZZA.

Fondue Night

Cheese sauce (pg. 137)

~

Salt and Pepper Shrimp with tempura dipping sauce (pg. 189)
or
9 Spice Chicken with honey balsamic glaze (pg. 76)
or
Steak au poivre with red wine sauce (pg. 98)

~

Strawberries with Chocolate Sauce (pg. 215)

I made this fondue menu specifically so people wouldn't have to shell out $150 at the restaurant we'll call Smelting Cot.

The only difficulty behind a fondue night is that for the entrée portion, the meat should be cooked through completely and simply coated with sauce as you are ready to eat. The shrimp, chicken and beef are all entrée options, so don't feel obligated to make everything. However, make sure that everything is bite size, so it will be easy to serve.

PREP ALL THE INGREDIENTS.

1. CHEESE SAUCE: Cheese is expensive, but this fondue is 1/8 of what it will cost if you were to go out. The one used by the best restaurants is called **comte'** (pronounced com-tay), which is a type of gruyere. **Fontina** is also great option, as well as **havarti** or even **pepper jack**- you just want something that melts well, with a bite. Try adding bacon for some smokiness, or even some cayenne pepper for some heat. For the cheese course, serve sliced apples, microwave blanched broccoli, slices of carrots and pieces of toasted French baguette (or simple breadsticks).

2. SHRIMP: Cook the shrimp at the last minute so they are hot because the dipping sauce is served at room temperature: it's very difficult to heat up soy sauce- based-sauces because soy sauce thickens when you increase the temperature, and there is a possibility of it burning.

   Serve them with this simple soy dipping sauce, which is made with ¾ cups of soy sauce to a ¼ cup of water, 1 teaspoon of sesame oil (optional), ¼ teaspoon of wasabi (or the equivalent amount made from wasabi powder mixed with a little water), 1 chopped scallion and 2 tablespoons of honey.

3. CHICKEN: Follow the recipe for the chicken. For the glaze, simply add 1 cup of balsamic vinegar to the pan on medium high heat. Allow it to cook down until the sauce forms a thick syrup, about 15 minutes. When the chicken is cooked, allow it to rest, then slice it in bite size pieces. Drizzle over the honey and balsamic glaze lightly over the chicken. *You don't want to coat the chicken like a barbecue sauce because the balsamic is very strong.*

4. BEEF: Follow the recipe for the *steak au poivre*. When the steak is cooked and has rested, slice it into bite size pieces. Using the pan drippings, deglaze the pan with 1 cup of red wine, 1 cup of beef stock and a dab of butter. Cook on high heat until the sauce has reduced by half, for about 10 minutes. In a small bowl, combine 1 tablespoon of flour with 1 tablespoon of butter with a fork. The butter and flour should clump together and form a small ball. Add it to the sauce, and whisk it in. It should thicken the sauce immediately

5. NUTELLA SAUCE: Buy one jar of Nutella and place it in a bowl. Add a couple tablespoons of milk and microwave it for 30 seconds. You want to thin the Nutella just enough so that it's the thickness of a chocolate syrup. Add a couple more tablespoons of milk and continue to cook in 30 second intervals. Heat up just before serving. Serve alongside sliced strawberries, bananas, store

bought doughnuts, or whatever you think would go well with chocolate.

We want to hear from you! Visit us at NewtonLocke.com, the Internet's Premiere Site for Undiscovered Talent, for news about upcoming events, updates on our artists and programs. To sign up for cooking lessons taught by Patrick, please email us.

BEST COLLEGE RECIPES WANTED! Send us your first and last name, the name of your school, a short story about your recipe, and the complete recipe and ingredients list to editors.thestinc@gmail.com for a chance to have your recipe featured in an upcoming volume of <u>Cooking for College Students</u>!

GET US INTO YOUR SCHOOL BOOKSTORE: Please help us get into your university bookstore. We offer special discounts to colleges and college students. Also keep a look out for the next volume of <u>Cooking for College Students</u>. Contact me at <u>www.thestinc.com</u> for more information.

Patrick C. Arenson is a college student and food enthusiast. He is the author of <u>The Little Boy Story</u> and is also the co-founder of <u>theStinc.com</u>, an online magazine for college students.

<u>Cooking for College Students: A Beginner's Guide</u> is the first volume of the Cooking for College Students Series.

9655887R00180

Printed in Great Britain
by Amazon.co.uk, Ltd.,
Marston Gate.